FRANCIS FRITH'S

LEICESTERSHIRE VILLAGES

PHOTOGRAPHIC MEMORIES

MICHAEL KILBURN was born and educated in Leicester before joining the Ancient Monuments Division of the Ministry of Public Buildings and Works. In 1970 he moved to the Historic Buildings Division of the Greater London Council and in 1986 to English Heritage as an Inspector of Historic Buildings (London Region). His other interests include the history of the landscape, lowland walking, Victorian theatre stage machinery, 18th-century music and jazz. His previous book is 'London's Theatres', an architectural study of fifty-three West End playhouses. Married with two sons, he now lives in South West Wales.

FRANCIS FRITH'S
PHOTOGRAPHIC MEMORIES

LEICESTERSHIRE VILLAGES

PHOTOGRAPHIC MEMORIES

MICHAEL KILBURN

First published in the United Kingdom in 2004 by
Frith Book Company Ltd

Hardback Edition 2004
ISBN 1-85937-655-X

British Library Cataloguing in Publication Data

Francis Frith's Leicestershire Villages - Photographic Memories
Michael Kilburn
ISBN 1-85937-655-X

Frith Book Company Ltd
Frith's Barn, Teffont,
Salisbury, Wiltshire SP3 5QP
Tel: +44 (0) 1722 716 376
Email: info@francisfrith.co.uk
www.francisfrith.co.uk

Printed and bound in Great Britain

Front Cover: **WOODHOUSE EAVES**, *View from Rocks c1960* W367075t
Frontispiece: **COSSINGTON**, *Main Street c1965* C470001

*The colour-tinting is for illustrative purposes only, and is not intended
to be historically accurate*

CONTENTS

FRANCIS FRITH
VICTORIAN PIONEER

FRANCIS FRITH, founder of the world-famous photographic archive, was a complex and multi-talented man. A devout Quaker and a highly successful Victorian businessman, he was philosophical by nature and pioneering in outlook.

By 1855 he had already established a wholesale grocery business in Liverpool, and sold it for the astonishing sum of £200,000, which is the equivalent today of over £15,000,000. Now a very rich man, he was able to indulge his passion for travel. As a child he had pored over travel books written by early explorers, and his fancy and imagination had been stirred by family holidays to the sublime mountain regions of Wales and Scotland. 'What lands of spirit-stirring and enriching scenes and places!' he had written. He was to return to these scenes of grandeur in later years to 'recapture the thousands of vivid and tender memories', but with a different purpose. Now in his thirties, and captivated by the new science of photography, Frith set out on a series of pioneering journeys up the Nile and to the Near East that occupied him from 1856 until 1860.

INTRIGUE AND EXPLORATION

These far-flung journeys were packed with intrigue and adventure. In his life story, written when he was sixty-three, Frith tells of being held captive by bandits, and of fighting 'an awful midnight battle to the very point of surrender with a deadly pack of hungry, wild dogs'. Wearing flowing Arab costume, Frith arrived at Akaba by camel sixty years before Lawrence of Arabia, where he encountered 'desert princes and rival sheikhs, blazing with jewel-hilted swords'.

He was the first photographer to venture beyond the sixth cataract of the Nile. Africa was still the mysterious 'Dark Continent', and Stanley and Livingstone's historic meeting was a decade into the future. The conditions for picture taking confound belief. He laboured for hours in his wicker dark-room in the sweltering heat of the desert, while the volatile chemicals fizzed dangerously in their trays. Back in London he exhibited his photographs and was 'rapturously cheered' by members of the Royal Society. His reputation as a photographer was made overnight.

VENTURE OF A LIFE-TIME

Characteristically, Frith quickly spotted the opportunity to create a new business as a specialist publisher of photographs. He lived in an era of immense and sometimes violent change.

For the poor in the early part of Victoria's reign work was exhausting and the hours long, and people had precious little free time to enjoy themselves. Most had no transport other than a cart or gig at their disposal, and rarely travelled far beyond the boundaries of their own town or village. However, by the 1870s the railways had threaded their way across the country, and Bank Holidays and half-day Saturdays had been made obligatory by Act of Parliament. All of a sudden the working man and his family were able to enjoy days out and see a little more of the world.

With typical business acumen, Francis Frith foresaw that these new tourists would enjoy having souvenirs to commemorate their days out. In 1860 he married Mary Ann Rosling and set out on a new career: his aim was to photograph every city, town and village in Britain. For the next thirty years he travelled the country by train and by pony and trap, producing fine photographs of seaside resorts and beauty spots that were keenly bought by millions of Victorians. These prints were painstakingly pasted into family albums and pored over during the dark nights of winter, rekindling precious memories of summer excursions.

THE RISE OF FRITH & CO

Frith's studio was soon supplying retail shops all over the country. To meet the demand he gathered about him a small team of photographers, and published the work of independent artist-photographers of the calibre of Roger Fenton and Francis Bedford. In order to gain some understanding of the scale of Frith's business one only has to look at the catalogue issued by Frith & Co in 1886: it runs to some 670 pages, listing not only many thousands of views of the British Isles but also many photographs of most European countries, and China, Japan, the USA and Canada - note the sample page shown on page 9 from the hand-written Frith & Co ledgers recording the pictures. By 1890 Frith had created the greatest specialist photographic publishing company in the world, with over 2,000 sales outlets - more than the combined number that Boots and WH Smith have today! The picture on the next page shows the Frith & Co display board at Ingleton in the Yorkshire Dales (left of window). Beautifully constructed with a mahogany frame and gilt inserts, it could display up to a dozen local scenes.

POSTCARD BONANZA

The ever-popular holiday postcard we know today took many years to develop. In 1870 the Post Office issued the first plain cards, with a pre-printed stamp on one face. In 1894 they allowed other publishers' cards to be sent through the mail with an attached adhesive halfpenny stamp. Demand grew rapidly, and in 1895 a new size of postcard was permitted called the court card, but there was little room for illustration. In 1899, a year after Frith's death, a new card measuring 5.5 x 3.5 inches became the standard format, but it was not until 1902 that the divided back came into being, so that the address and message could be on one face and a full-size illustration on the other. Frith & Co were in the vanguard of postcard development: Frith's sons Eustace and Cyril continued their father's monumental task, expanding the number of views offered to the public and recording more and more places in Britain, as the coasts and countryside were opened up to mass travel.

Francis Frith had died in 1898 at his villa in Cannes, his great project still growing. The archive he created continued in business for another seventy years. By 1970 it contained over a third of a million pictures showing 7,000 British towns and villages.

FRANCIS FRITH'S LEGACY

Frith's legacy to us today is of immense significance and value, for the magnificent archive of evocative photographs he created provides a unique record of change in the cities, towns and villages throughout Britain over a century and more. Frith and his fellow studio photographers revisited locations many times down the years to update their views, compiling for us an enthralling and colourful pageant of British life and character.

We are fortunate that Frith was dedicated to recording the minutiae of everyday life. For it is this sheer wealth of visual data, the painstaking chronicle of changes in dress, transport, street layouts, buildings, housing, engineering and landscape that captivates us so much today. His remarkable images offer us a powerful link with the past and with the lives of our ancestors.

THE VALUE OF THE ARCHIVE TODAY

Computers have now made it possible for Frith's many thousands of images to be accessed almost instantly. Frith's images are increasingly used as visual resources, by social historians, by researchers into genealogy and ancestry, by architects and town planners, and by teachers involved in local history projects.

In addition, the archive offers every one of us an opportunity to examine the places where we and our families have lived and worked down the years. Highly successful in Frith's own era, the archive is now, a century and more on, entering a new phase of popularity. Historians consider the Francis Frith Collection to be of prime national importance. It is the only archive of its kind remaining in private ownership. Francis Frith's archive is now housed in an historic timber barn in the beautiful village of Teffont in Wiltshire. Its founder would not recognize the archive office as it is today. In place of the many thousands of dusty boxes containing glass plate negatives and an all-pervading odour of photographic chemicals, there are now ranks of computer screens. He would be amazed to watch his images travelling round the world at unimaginable speeds through internet lines.

The archive's future is both bright and exciting. Francis Frith, with his unshakeable belief in making photographs available to the greatest number of people, would undoubtedly approve of what is being done today with his lifetime's work. His photographs depicting our shared past are now bringing pleasure and enlightenment to millions around the world a century and more after his death.

LEICESTERSHIRE VILLAGES
AN INTRODUCTION

'I want to speak of the unknown Midland country that lies between here (Warwickshire) and the fens, fifty miles away, the most generally unknown tract of country of any size in the whole of England'.

W G Hoskins
'Midland England' 1949

FEW authors before or since W G Hoskins, the pioneer of English Landscape Studies, with perhaps the exception of Maurice Beresford and Christopher Taylor, have demonstrated the breadth of knowledge and the almost poetic literary skills which combined to provide Hoskins's three-dimensional view of Leicestershire and the Midlands in 'Midland England', followed in 1955 by his seminal work 'The Making of the English Landscape'. His observation quoted above could have been written fifty years later, as Leicestershire and Rutland continue to be best known for a football team that yo-yos between the Premier League and Division One, and a fading cricket team, but for little else. In the mid 20th century, Leicester was acknowledged world-wide through famous names such as Imperial typewriters, Pex socks, Chilprufe children's wear and Wadkins Engineering: all have gone.

Over more recent years, Hoskins' joy in the variety and visual beauty of Leicestershire and Rutland has been exchanged by many archaeologists and historians for computerised facts of amazing technical accuracy. Specialists will provide Carbon-14 and tree-ring dating, 'historic landscape characterisations', and 'time depths', with little or no hint of the beauty of hawthorn in bloom, or the colour as the evening sun strikes the church and houses of an ironstone village in 'high' Leicestershire or Rutland.

Even the city that Hoskins knew and loved (apart from its central historic core, which survives in mainly 18th-century streets, grouped around the cathedral and medieval Guildhall) has, since the 1950s, been reduced to a spectacularly uncoordinated architectural wilderness, particularly on its north and east sides. The first outer ring of villages, including Belgrave, Evington (which does retain its green), Aylestone, and Humberstone, have been subsumed into the city's suburban expansion. In the case of Humberstone, the recent Hamilton Estate Development pushes northwards into an attractive enclosure landscape, as it drops away to the deserted medieval village site of Hamilton, one of the finest in the county. Further out, villages such as Houghton-on-the-Hill have, to a limited extent, felt the first breeze of change as development turns up on the doorstep.

Next to be targeted by the County Council as ripe for 'development' will, as usual, be the commuter villages such as Billesdon, close to the city, yet in the country. These villages will be more and more vulnerable to surreptitious attack, firstly by the provision of backland infill, and then by piecemeal development that nibbles away almost imperceptibly at the historic outer fringe, particularly of a nucleated settlement. Listing buildings of special architectural or historic interest ensures their statutory protection, but designated Conservation Area status sounds much more protective than it really is. Vigilance is essential, and developers with reassuring conservation-orientated names should be handled with care.

Leicestershire is not a large county, only some 40 miles by 40 at its extremes, while Rutland, England's smallest county, is roughly 15 miles by 17, with a population of a little in excess of 30,000 - hardly enough to provide a City football crowd on a good Saturday. Tilton-on-the-Hill is said (perhaps half jokingly) to be the coldest village in the county, as nothing stands between it and the Russian Urals. My father spent his boyhood in the early years of the 20th century living in the village and in nearby self-descriptive Cold Newton, and he would often chillingly subscribe to that adage.

The two counties cannot be said to be a magnet for tourism, notwithstanding the beauty of the ironstone and limestone villages of 'high' (East) Leicestershire and Rutland, which in many cases rival those of the better known Shakespeare Country or the Cotswolds. On the west side of the county, Charnwood Forest and Bradgate Park remain very much pleasure grounds, somehow reserved for Leicester people, as they always have been.

Having bemoaned the fate of the city and its peripheral settlements, a quiet day's walking out of Scraptoft, about four miles from the city

TILTON-ON-THE-HILL, *The Village c1955* T236007

centre on its east side, is to enter the rich world of concentrated landscape history which extends over much of 'high' Leicestershire and Rutland. Covert Lane, the extension of Scraptoft Lane, the original medieval Leicester to Stamford road, runs down past Monks Grave, an adulterine castle to Ingarsby, deserted in 1469. Then it goes past the long-closed Ingarsby railway station, and on to Quenby with its splendid Hall of 1620 and village earthworks of 1485, constructed about the time the Battle of Bosworth was raging on the west side of the county. Close by is Cold Newton, buried in medieval ridge and furrow, overlaid by enclosure hedgerows of the late 18th and early 19th centuries, home in 1800 to 101 people, and now reduced to one or two cottages and farmhouses. Then we walk north to deserted Loseby and to Baggrave, each sitting in its village earthworks, to return via Hungerton and Keyham to Scraptoft.

The photographs in this book are part of an extremely comprehensive and important record of the fabric of villages in Leicestershire and Rutland between two fixed points in time, from 1955 to 1965, a period when vast sociological and architectural changes were taking place. By 1955, we were shaking off the dust of austerity. Sweet rationing had ended in 1953, and we experienced the pleasure of seeing the Coronation, usually on a neighbour's television, that same year. In 1956 'The Home of Tomorrow' could be acquired in Crawley New Town, Sussex, for £2,200, at the same time that Le Corbusier was telling us that high-rise blocks of flats, his 'machines for living in', were our inescapable future! The 1960s delivered free love, the contraceptive pill, the Rolling Stones and the Beatles, a very young Twiggy, motorways and the rather

telling saying that 'if you remember the 60s you weren't there'. At the end of our period, 'Supermac', Harold Macmillan, was telling us that we'd never had it so good, and for better or worse, People Power was emerging.

Some two thirds of the churches included in this collection have spires, and although this could be said to be a limited sample (about 15% of the total number of parish churches in the two counties), it does show why that in the rolling open country of Leicestershire and Rutland the local saying is that 'one is never out of sight of a steeple'. To follow up on this by confirming that steeplechasing originated locally would seem almost logical, but in fact this was an Irish invention. In 1752 the first challenge was made, and the first race was run between the villages of Butterant and Donerail, about 30 miles north of Cork on the Awbeg river.

Leicestershire did, however, gain some kudos when in 1810 the first English racecourse, with its eight 4'6" fences, opened at Bedford: entries were accepted only from owners of horses that had taken part in a Leicestershire hunt, and been in at the kill - nothing less was acceptable.

Whether one loves it, hates it, or is indifferent to it, fox hunting (which developed in the later 17th century) played an inexorable part in the evolution of the landscape. Indeed, it boosted the economy of many villages, particularly to the east of the Soar Valley, from Hose in the north, to Swinford and Stanford Hall in the south. Melton Mowbray, Market Harborough and Oakham will always be remembered whatever their hunting future as world-famous centres, and nowhere other than in The Shires can there be a group of hunts to match in quality the Quorn, the Belvoir (formed around 1730), the Pytchley, Mr Fernie's

Hunt, the Cottesmore, and to the south-west the Atherstone, immortalised by Siegfried Sassoon in his 'Memoirs of a Fox Hunting Man', first published in 1937.

I have divided the counties into five convenient, loosely circular 'tours', using the north-south Soar Valley as a natural divide, and on the east side of Leicestershire the A47 Uppingham Road, with to the west a more arbitrary, but matching, line. Each tour will provide a surprising variation in not only the landscape, but also in the fabric of the villages. There will be obvious, inescapable changes in the look of villages in the early 21st century when compared to that same scene viewed through the camera lens in the decade under scrutiny. These changes are caused basically, it must be said, by the increase in living standards, and the consequent pressure, often to the detriment of the environment, either to encourage spending or to control the motor car.

Picturesque buildings have been demolished and replaced by the fashionable 'developers'

Georgian', neat shop fronts are almost obliterated by a profusion of 'two for the price of one' notices, and timber windows and doors have given way to the ubiquitous plastic. Yellow lines are to be seen almost everywhere, often accompanied by the ghastly speed humps and parking meters, and street furniture sprouts almost overnight while fast food containers blow about in the gutter. These are but a few detrimental changes that have taken place, and one has to regretfully say that it is difficult to cite visual changes for the better.

Melton Mowbray is the ideal centre from which to explore the Wolds, and also 'high' Leicestershire, that superb area whose hilly character is moulded by the oolitic limestone and marlstone or ironstone belts sweeping up from Dorset into Yorkshire. (The meaning of 'Wold' or 'Wald' is uncertain. Early Anglo-Saxon writings imply a lack of woodland, while after the turn of the 13th century, a wooded landscape is suggested). Melton Mowbray is, of course, the home of the world-famous pork pie, although

FLECKNEY, *The Grand Union Canal c1965* F134022

the original recipe, which included currants, raisins, and anchovies, has been considerably modified over the years.

There is much red brick as well as stone to be seen in the south-eastern quadrant of Leicestershire around Market Harborough. The town grew up as a market centre at the crossing of the river Welland around 1175, within the parish of Great Bowden - hence the town centre church has no graveyard, and no burial rights. The Grand Union Canal winds its way south from Foxton into the terminus basin on the north side of the town, and the Welland Valley stretches away north-eastwards towards Stamford, through fine meadowland, passing a series of attractive villages including Bringhurst, Great Easton, Caldecott, Cottingham and Rockingham at its southern end. The first railway station was built here in 1850, with huntsmen worrying about an excess of water and the railway - all without foundation. T F Dale (in 'Fox Hunting in the Shires', 1903) summed up the town beautifully when he wrote 'Market Harborough is a pleasant old town with the grace of antiquity clinging to it'.

Chapter 3 contains our series of photographs covering Rutland; by the placing of the selected villages on the map, it affords a first-rate opportunity to cover the county. Travelling in the south, say, from Caldecott to Seaton, it is almost obligatory to visit the Norman church at Stoke Dry and the Bishop of Lincoln's Bede House at Lyddington; or further north, the parish church of St Peter and St Paul at Exton with its wonderful collection of monumental sculpture, and Burley-on-the-Hill, beckon on the journey from Cottesmore to Langham.

In its early history, Rutland was something of an outlier to the Middle Angles' headquarters at Leicester. Later in 1002, it appears that King Ethelred gave what was in effect a Saxon estate to his queen, Emma, initiating a long association between the county and royalty. With so much to see, excellent overnight accommodation is to be had in the county's market towns of Oakham and Uppingham, both home to notable public schools. Oh yes, and don't forget that visit to Rutland Water!

The north-western part of the county, our Chapter 4, is centred on Loughborough, and it is an area of stark contrasts between the beauty of Bradgate Park, Groby Pool and Swithland, and the dour industrial, red brick, clay-based landscape of the remainder. Villages such as Shepshed became famous for worsted framework knitting, along with its brickworks. Groby and Mountsorrel were producing granite, and Swithland slate, until this industry was wiped out by cheap, lightweight, easily riven Welsh slates - and now we have concrete tiles!

Bardon Hill and Breedon Hill are disfigured by the insatiable appetite for endless quarrying. Coal has been mined in the area (and also in south Derbyshire) since medieval times, and Snibston No 2 Pit, which closed some twenty years ago, is now a museum to mining known as Snibston Discovery Park.

Some seven miles to the west of Coalville is Moira, developed as an industrial village in the early 19th century by the Irish Earls of Moira, who erected a smelting furnace here around 1805. The ironstone in the area turned out to be poor, which caused the furnace to close rather abruptly before 1815. The furnace, its adjacent cottages and associated kilns, which remain in situ, is a scheduled Ancient Monument, setting it alongside the Bedlam Furnaces at Ironbridge.

So many villages have coal engraved into their very fabric, with the stories of many lives lived hard in the mines, and indeed, in the quarries. Long before sunrise on a quiet winter's morning, the click of the blakies might still be heard on the metalled roadway - or is it just imagination?

Lastly, this volume looks at the area around Hinckley, built on the clay lands known as the Leicestershire Plain, which until the development of turnpike roads was the bane of travellers' lives. Daniel Defoe in the early 18th century referred to the clay as 'so surprisingly soft, that it is perfectly frightful to travellers ... indeed a great number of horses were killed by excessive labour in those hard ways'.

Hinckley is not a beautiful town, but it does hold the distinction that a knitting frame was working here in 1640 (the first outside London); and by the later 18th century there were approaching 900 such frames. Factories survive in the town, including those around Lower and Upper Bond Street and Hill Street. Close by, Earl Shilton and Barwell, also framework knitting centres, diversified into the boot and shoe industry.

Within this area is the attractive town of Market Bosworth, close to Ambien Hill. Here, on 22 August 1485, King Richard III was successfully challenged for the English throne by Henry Tudor, later King Henry VII. Richard was killed in the fighting, and buried at Greyfriars, Leicester. The site of the battle is open to the public, and it is extremely well exhibited.

Sir James Musgrave summed up Quorn Country thus at the end of the great run of 1832: 'Just ten miles as the crow flies, in one hour and ten minutes, with but two trifling checks, over the finest country in the world'. I feel that the whole of our two counties at the start of the 21st century are indeed 'the finest country in the world'.

TWYCROSS, *St James' Church c1955* T237007

MELTON MOWBRAY AND THE WOLDS

'Among the taller wood with ivy hung,
The old fox plays and dances round her young,
She snuffs and barks if any passes by
And swings her tail and turns prepared to fly.'

John Clare
'The Vixen' 1835

TILTON-ON-THE-HILL, *The Village c1955* T236007

Some eight miles south of Melton Mowbray, Loddington Road rises to the parish church of St Peter, the high point of the county's highest village at about 700 feet. The main Market Harborough to Melton Mowbray road sweeps away on its west side. The railway, now only an earthwork a mile to the east, arrived in 1879, to be used in transporting ironstone away from the open-cast quarries in the north-east of the parish. The surrounding area was once more densely populated, as the deserted medieval villages of Marefield, Whatborough and Loseby, and the shrunken village of Cold Newton, demonstrate.

TILTON-ON-THE-HILL
The Rose and Crown
c1955 P236011

Traditionally sited next to the churchyard, the Rose and Crown is a good, real ale pub. With the new European Union safety regulations relating to leaning gravestones coming into force, we can say goodbye to the romantic views we have known all our lives. The juxtaposition of pub to church was beautifully summed up by George Herbert in his 'Jacula Prudentum' (1640): 'no sooner is a temple built to God, but the Devil builds a Chapel hard by'.

TILTON-ON-THE-HILL, *St Peter's Church c1955* T236010

St Peter's was originally late Norman, but virtually rebuilt in the 15th century. It is notable for its collection of grotesque gargoyles, and for two carved capitals which are derived from the stories of Reynard the Fox; appropriate in Cottesmore country. The church was restored in 1854 by Richard Charles Hussey of Birmingham (1802-1887). In 1835 he became a partner of the great Thomas Rickman (1776-1841), the first man to divide the medieval periods into Norman, Early English, Decorated and Perpendicular. On the left, the 'Gothic' school has been badly treated above its ground storey.

LITTLE DALBY, *St James' Church c1955* L32060

The church sits in a well-treed landscape, close to the basically late 16th-century Hall of the Hartopp family, who financed the building of the church in 1851. This rather ponderous Victorian Gothic building, designed by Raphael Brandon (1817-77), is faced in ironstone, with a heavy spire and tower. The fixtures and fittings are all of 1852, including some stained glass by Augustus Welby Pugin. Brandon was a versatile architect of some merit, equally at home designing St Mary's Church, Humberside (1857), or the tower and spire of Leicester Cathedral. In 1730 Mrs Orton ensured the village's undying fame, for although she sold it at Stilton in Huntingdonshire, it was here that she created Stilton cheese.

▲ BURTON LAZARS
St James' Church c1955 B890057

Here was the Hospital of St Mary and St Lazarus of Jerusalem, founded by Robert de Mowbray in the mid-12th century. It was the premier leper colony in medieval England, with a master, eight brothers and leper brethren. Extensive earthworks on the south-west side of the village mark its site. The ironstone church has a slightly odd saddleback double bellcote, but the churchyard exhibits a number of good headstones, including one to Mary Blower of 1781 by Christopher Staveley, a Melton Mowbray builder, with a lovely relief of Charity. The spectacular monument in the photograph was erected to weaver William Squire in 1781.

◄ **DETAIL FROM** B890057

19

SAXBY, *St Peter's Church c1955* S546002

St Peters was designed by architect George Richardson in 1789 (for Robert Sherrard, 4th Earl of Harborough) in the Classical manner that Pevsner describes as 'an attempt at combining the tradition of Hawksmoor churches of London with Leicestershire usage'. The finest feature is its tower with angle volutes and vases crowned by a slim spire. Not only did the 4th Earl build at Saxby, he also commissioned St Mary Magdalen, Stapleford, and Holy Trinity, Teigh. The 4th Earl, known as the building Earl, enlarged Stapleford Hall, the ancestral home, built a bridge at Melton Mowbray, and the Town Hall at Market Harborough.

SAXBY, *St Peter's Church, the Nave c1955* S546001

George Richardson's early career was spent as a draughtsman in the office of Robert and James Adam, and indeed he was a fine interior designer in the Adam style, providing a number of drawings for Kedleston Hall in the late 1760s. In the photograph, clear glass illuminates not Richardson's interior, but the soulless one created by Joseph Goddard (see St Andrew's, Countesthorpe) in 1874. He replaced the original ceiling, lowered the floor, and installed heavy, off-the-peg pews - a thoroughly bad job by a talented architect.

21

▼ **FREEBY,** *St Mary's Church c1955* F22050

This is a pretty church in a small village to the north east of Melton Mowbray, on what was once a route through to Sproxton. Earthworks around the village, including a sunken way to the north, speak of a larger medieval settlement. The pinnacled tower, faced in limestone, is of the 15th century, while the body of the church was built in ironstone a century earlier.

▶ **BELVOIR CASTLE** *1890*
27852

Here is a wonderfully atmospheric shot, typical of the best of late 19th-century photography, illustrating the beautiful view from which Belvoir derives its name. The castle was first recorded in 1130 as Beleder; the building seen today is a remodelling in yellow ironstone by architect James Wyatt in 1801 for the 5th Duchess of Rutland. Beyond the thick wooded cover, the more open land of the deer park is corrugated by the medieval ridge and furrow of open field cultivation. In the foreground, the cottages are roofed in attractive pantiles, a common material in this part of the county.

◄ BOTTESFORD
Market Street
c1955 B515010

On the A52 between Nottingham and Grantham, Bottesford is the most northerly settlement in the county. An expansive village, it sits on the River Devon, about a mile north of the Grantham Canal of 1797. This view looks south, away from the church. On the left is the base of the stepped 14th-century cross, which retains the eroded arms of the de Roos family, a number of whom are buried in the church, including Robert de Roos (1285) and William, Lord Roos (1414). The historic village centre peters out beyond the right-hand turn into the High Street.

► BOTTESFORD
Market Street c1960
B514004

St Mary's Church dominates the village and the surrounding countryside. The historic core is arranged around the churchyard, including the early 18th-century rectory and Fleming's Bridge, named after an early 17th-century rector, built c1620. Fleming's Almshouses (left), also of c1620, were rebuilt c1750 as cottages. Being well known in the area probably means that Mr Bugg, the family butcher (left), does not urgently need to repaint his deteriorating gable-end sign!

BOTTESFORD, *St Mary's Church, the Earl of Rutland's Monument 1890* 22861

Approach from the south, over a brook and through trees, to the 15th-century tower and slender recessed crocketed spire of St Mary's, standing over 200 feet high. However, it is not the architecture that attracts visitors here, it is the magnificent series of monuments to the Roos family of the 15th century and above all to eight Earls of Rutland, ranging from 1543 to 1679. The monument in the photograph commemorates the 2nd Earl, who died in 1563. A lively tomb, it has the Earl and his wife lying under a domestic-looking table, upon which are kneeling figures and a vertical armorial slab.

HOSE
The Village c1955 H358013

On the north-east side of the county, Hose is situated close to the Nottinghamshire border in the Vale of Belvoir. The village sits astride an ancient, pre-Roman trackway which ran from Burrough Camp, some six miles south of Melton Mowbray, into Nottinghamshire, with to its south the escarpment of the Wolds. The Grantham-Nottingham Canal of 1793 runs through the parish, and a wharf once served the village. The photograph, taken on the edge of the green and close to the church, records rather mundane, red brick buildings under pantiled roofs, along with a rather more interesting chestnut tree.

HOSE, *The Black Horse, Bolton Lane c1955* H358014

In a not unattractive red brick, end-of-village group, it is impossible not to notice the Black Horse pub, with its well-mannered frontage and attractive pantiled roofs. The cantilevered pub sign over the front door advertises Home Ales from the Home Brewery in Nottingham, now a cog in Scottish & Newcastle's big wheel, but still producing good real ale.

► **HOSE**
The Village c1955
H358007

At the junction immediately to the south-east of the village stands a prefabricated bungalow, upon which much love has been lavished. The Harby to Stathern road runs off the photograph to the right, and on that road are the earthworks of an outlying grange of Croxden Abbey, along with a windmill mound in the aptly named Mill Field. Croxden is a Cistercian foundation of 1176, situated in Staffordshire. The very fine, substantial remains are in the care of English Heritage.

◄ **HOSE**
St Michael's Church c1955 H358015

Overlooking the green on the south side of the village, the church is large, but lacks any architectural get-up-and-go! It is of the 14th century, and faced in ironstone with some aged brickwork; the high limestone clerestory presents a dominant feature. An interesting feature is the large octagonal font, ornamented with angels with outstretched wings.

▲ **SCALFORD,** *The Church of St Egelwin the Martyr, interior c1955* S253013

The basic fabric of the church can be no later than the end of the Early English period, around 1300. The elegant five-bay north and south arcades are witness to this date. One of two 14th-century tomb recesses with ball-flower decoration can be seen between columns to the left. The excellent west tower was built in 1649. The chancel was rebuilt in 1858 by the architects Millican & Smith, who also carried out unremarkable works at Arnesby, Bagworth and Markfield, among others.

◄**AB KETTLEBY**
St James' Church c1955
A357039

On the exposed Wolds, the ironstone church is situated on the south side of the village street, away from the main A606 Nottingham to Stamford road. Here, in a relatively elaborate tomb, lies Everard Digby, who died in 1628, namesake of Sir Everard, who was executed for his part in the Gunpowder Plot in 1605. The weathered stonework of the church is mainly of the 13th century, with a later very elegant spire, all over-restored in 1852 by local builders Broadbent & Hawley.

THORPE ARNOLD
St Mary's Church
c1955 T234001

In a well-treed setting, the church is seen from the west. This small elevated village lies about a mile to the north-east of Melton Mowbray on the A607 Grantham road. There are earthworks to the south-west of the church, the remains of what appears to be a 17th-century formal garden, and eroded house platforms along the south side of the road. The church tower was rebuilt in 1875 by R W Johnson.

THORPE ARNOLD, *St Mary's Church, the Nave c1955* T234002

This view from the nave looking east into the chancel is not exciting, nor is it enhanced by the solid fuel heating pipes to left and right. The chancel arch was rebuilt by Johnson, a Melton Mowbray architect, who achieved little of note. His work appears to have been virtually confined to the immediate area, which may be just as well! The font (right, through the south arcade arch) is 12th-century, and decorated with rather naive yet animated carvings of dragons, and a sword-wielding St George. Also of importance are the corbels in the nave, which may also be of early date.

SAXELBY, *St Peter's Church c1955* S705053

The not unlovely village of Saxelby is situated about a mile north of industrial Asfordby, and on a stream which empties into the River Wreake. It has a good selection of ironstone houses and farmhouses, but to the east of the church the settlement has retreated, leaving a series of earthworks to mark its former presence. This wintry shot of the 13th-century ironstone church looks from the south east at the dominant 15th-century tower and its recessed crocketed spire. The chancel (right) and the south porch were rebuilt in 1856 by an unknown hand.

29

▶ **SAXELBY,** *St Peter's Church, the Nave c1955* S705054

The view looks down the nave and into the chancel with the rather fine four-bay arcade of about 1300 to the right. The south aisle window (right) is of the 15th century, and the fine pulpit to the left of the chancel arch is of a century later. There is a modest selection of brass and slate monuments, including an incised slab to Robert Brokesby (1531).

▼ **ASFORDBY,** *The River Wreake and the Church c1955* A211004

Three miles to the west of Melton Mowbray, the photographer stood on the triple-arched medieval and later bridge to the south-west of All Saints' Church to capture what appears to be a haven of reedy tranquillity in an industrialised landscape. Out of sight to the right is all the ugliness of Stanton and Staveley's iron producing furnaces, built in 1878 and shut down in 1958.

▶ **ASFORDBY**
The Old Hall, Main Street c1955
A211011

Situated at the western end of the village is the Old Hall, formerly the Manor House, a building of considerable grace and charm dating from around 1620. Faced in a weather-beaten rendered red brick under a triple gable, the two stories of sashed windows are some 150 years later. The originals are likely to have been cross casements. Internally, some Jacobean woodwork survives, as does a wooden spiral back stair.

▶ **ASFORDBY**
Dalgleish Way
c1965 A211018

Dalgleish Way is part of the later 1950s and early 1960s village expansion. We are looking towards Mill Lane, with comfortable but typically uninspired housing of a sort to be found on the edge of many Leicestershire towns and villages. Although lacking hedges and trees, the gardens are maturing behind fences and dwarf walls. The local council has already made a start on digging up the road and footpaths.

31

▲ ASFORDBY
All Saints' Church and the Rectory
c1955 A211009

This wonderful photograph could be used to illustrate any romantic 19th-century novel. At the end of Church Lane to the west of All Saints' Church the base of a medieval cross survives with its new shaft and head of the 1920s. Inside the church, remnants of a carved Saxon cross depicting a dragon and a priest are built into the south aisle. The building is impressive: tower and crocketed spire is 15th-century, while the body is of the 14th century. Some reused Norman stones survive in what appears to be a small Easter Sepulchre. The red brick rectory dates from about 1810.

▶ **DETAIL FROM** A211009

FRISBY-ON-THE-WREAKE, *The Church of St Thomas of Canterbury c1955* F241014

An attractive village south of the railway line and the River Wreake, Frisby has a number of good houses. It was originally on the main Leicester/Melton Mowbray road until 1810, when Edward Parsons, who also put in the turnpike at Kibworth, built what amounts to a two-mile bypass from Rotherby to Chalk Pool Hill. The church, a Norman foundation, is impressive, dominated by its ironstone tower and recessed spire. The main body of the church is 14th-century, but the chancel was rebuilt in 1848 by H J Stevens, a prolific Derby architect. The south transept is the high point of any visit with its very beautiful curvilinear traceried window (right).

▶ **BURTON ON THE WOLDS**
Seymour Road c1960
B516003

This small village, about three miles to the east of Loughborough, has in recent decades expanded to accommodate country-dwelling commuters. One building of interest is the Hall, mainly of the late 18th century, which was formerly the hunting lodge for the Dukes of Somerset. A small mission church in the village is dependent on St Andrews, Prestwold. The photograph clearly illustrates the village expansion with housing that could literally be anywhere.

◄ BURTON ON THE WOLDS
The Post Office and the Square c1960 B516004

Next to an 18th century house of some interest, the post office, along with the pub, was the focal point of village life. The need to collect the pension and perhaps a few postage stamps could be spiced up with a little discreet local gossip. Now, thanks to cut-backs, post offices disappear like ghosts into the night. To the east of the village are the earthworks of a moated grange to Garendon Abbey, a Cistercian house founded in 1377.

BURTON ON THE WOLDS
The Greyhound Inn
c1960 B516026

This rather imposing white-painted late 18th- or early 19th-century brick-faced pub under a slated roof is set back from the main village street, selling Shipstones Ales from a local Nottingham brewery founded by James Shipstone in 1852. He controlled the enterprise for close on thirty years, but like so many others, in 1978 Shipstones merged with Greenall Whitney, a very large concern, brewing in Warrington, Lancashire.

BARROW-UPON-SOAR, *The Bridge and the River c1960* B514005

The cows are lying down, a sure sign of rain, the old saying goes, but whether this is true or false they add a picturesque finishing touch to a watery scene. Situated about 8 miles north of Leicester, by Domesday 'Barhou' was settled. Today, it is the river and the lime works which are the village's most valuable assets. The lime produced here is considered to be of the finest quality.

BARROW-UPON-SOAR
The River c1955
B514003

For many years the river at Barrow has possessed a watery magnetism which has drawn people from the city to its banks on warm summer days, either to enjoy a picnic, or to venture onto the water in a variety of craft. It is regrettable that in our increasingly litigious 21st century, where a stubbed toe or a sprained ankle can cost boat hire firms dear in compensation, simple boating pleasures may be slowly but surely drawing to a close.

BARROW-UPON-SOAR, *High Street and the Village Sign c1965* B514025

This traffic island at the south end of the High Street, with its random stone walling, double yellow lines, and Festival of Britain-style sign, somehow epitomises a rather unlovely village. Even the church of Holy Trinity, masked here by the foreground tree, was built in forbidding Mountsorrel granite c1865 by Derbyshire architects, Stevens & Robinson. Internally, there is a mid 17th-century monument to Theophilus Cave in the chancel, and one from the mid 18th century to Martha Utber in the south transept.

▶ **BARROW-UPON-SOAR**
High Street c1965
B514028

The camera looks north-south along the High Street as it crosses the Leicester to Nottingham railway, and at a not unattractive group of houses and shops ranging in date from the 18th century to modern. The modern intrusions, such as Kinsell's electrical shop and the adjacent post office (left), do little to enhance the group. Surviving K6 telephone kiosks (left) are now of historic interest, being designed by Sir Giles Gilbert Scott in 1935, based on the tomb of architect Sir John Soane at St Giles-in-the-Fields (1616).

◀ **BARROW-UPON-SOAR**
Humphrey Perkin's School, Cotes Road c1955 B514015

These restrained yet assured buildings, designed in the manner of C P A Voysey, were a part of the City and County network of superb grammar schools. The County Architect, T A Collins, designed extensions to the group in 1955, and 'Bird Watching', a concrete sculpture by Peter Peri, was commissioned to enliven the composition.

▲ **SILEBY,** *Seagrave Road c1965* S498014

This is a red (probably local) brick, typically Midland boot and shoe and hosiery village east of Sileby Lock, on the Grand Union Canal. The church of St Mary is impressive, particularly the 14th-century tower. K G Cowling's maltings and brewery makes an impact; of the domestic architecture, interest is mainly confined to the Free Trade Inn of c1600, and a number of 18th-century weavers' cottages. These houses stepping down into the village are enhanced by their original features, especially their timber double-hung sash windows. By the turn of the 21st century, the double-glazing salesmen will have been calling.

◄**SILEBY,** *The Entrance To The Memorial Gardens c1960* S498004

Following the armistice in 1918, war memorials were erected by many parishes throughout the British Isles, either close to the church, or in a public place, as a symbol of a shared grief, where people could come together to remember their relatives and friends. Gardens such as this should also be able to offer a private area where it is possible to reflect quietly, away from public gaze, but this is often a rare luxury. At Sileby in 1960 the approach to the garden is somewhat grim, with only a few shrubs and an isolated tree.

▼ **SILEBY** *The Memorial Gardens c1960* S498002

Regimented pollard trees do little to provide a backdrop screen which will mask out the endless row of unattractive house backs, against which the memorial tends to be lost. The immediate area is, of course, ideal for open air services, but the 'no cycling' sign has nothing to add to the scene.

► **SILEBY**
The Greedon Estate c1965
S498011

The Greedon Estate is situated on the north west side of the Seagrave Road. This is a particularly uninspiring view, but again it is a view so typical of peripheral village estates. Concrete post and wire fences and rough grass verges do little to help the scene, but G and E Jackson & Son Ltd's shop front, so typical of the 1950s, just adds the dire finishing touch to the scene.

◀ **SILEBY**
Barrow Road
c1965 S498010

The view looks at St Mary's from the north, along a varied terrace of possibly late 18th- and 19th-century houses which are not enhanced by the long brick boundary wall. So far as the church tower is concerned, it is almost good enough to be in the West Country. However, the body of the building is modest, with a faithful partial restoration in 1878 by Sir Arthur Blomfield (1829-99), whose major work was the rebuilding of the nave and south transept to Southwark Cathedral.

▶ **COSSINGTON**
Main Street c1965
C470001

This is an oasis between industrial Syston and unlovely Sileby, where, apart from an increase in traffic, the scene has changed little. In the village are a good variety of houses, including the early 16th-century rectory, and Hallside Grove, a Gothicised house of quality. On the left is a simple but attractive farmhouse in a peaceful well-treed rural villagescape, built about the time that Jane Austen was writing. Immediately beyond, modern infill points to a commuter dormitory scenario.

SYSTON
High Street
c1955 S488008

This is an attractive corner of 'Sithestan', as Syston was known in 1254. The house forming the angle with Chapel Street on the left dates from before the 17th century. The late 19th-century Bull's Head is now a part of Allied Breweries of Burton-upon-Trent. As is so common, over half the buildings in the middle distance have gone, to make way for unattractive 1960s and 70s replacements. Adjacent to the thatched house is an excellent early 19th-century three-storey red brick residence which overlooks The Green on its south side.

SYSTON
The Green c1955
S488009

The 15th-century local granite and limestone church tower of St Peter and St Paul, heavily restored in 1872 by P W Ordish, shows above the houses of quality which bound The Green. It must have been a considerable worry at Council meetings when plans were discussed for the transformation of this attractive open area. So, instead of being a sensitive pedestrian and architecturally friendly scheme, the area is now a peculiarly urban villagescape, half car park and half odd seating which one would hesitate to use. All-in-all, it blends, I suppose, with the remainder of this unfortunate village.

◄ **SYSTON**
*High Street
c1955* S488012

In a scene little changed since the 1920s, a rather choleric lion gazes down the Melton Road from his elevated position on the strangely classical war memorial. All the buildings are typical of their date, but later alterations and rebuilding have eroded their quality. The memorial with its lion was removed in the later 1960s to make way for a mini roundabout, and now resides on a less obstructive site close to the British Legion.

▲ **SYSTON,** *High Street c1965* S488041

The buildings of the mid 1960s loom large here (centre), and the once red brick Bull's Head glows white in its new livery. Next to the Bull's Head is a small early 20th-century building, and next to this a mundane Co-operative shop is transformed by its fine contemporary timber shop front. So few have been allowed to survive in the never-ending quest for more glazing; whether this sells more bags of sugar or boxes of soap powder is questionable.

◄ **SYSTON**
Broad Street c1955 S488004

Syston was industrialised by an influx of framework knitters in the 19th century, whose typical architectural legacy was standardised red brick buildings of neat design. After the Second World War the village was devastated by planning ineptness, causing W G Hoskins to refer to it as a 'large and ugly industrial village'. The photograph exhibits some of the architectural harmony at the junction of Broad Street with Melton Road. Bicycles lean casually against the fence, no double yellow lines - memories of yesteryear, gone beyond recall!

▶ **THURMASTON**
St Michael's Church c1965 T235004

St Michael's stands on the east side of Melton Road in the centre of the village. Only the tower remains from the early 14th-century; the remainder was rebuilt using some original materials by Henry Stevens of Derby in 1848, who also restored a number of churches on the west side of the county. The two rather grand foreground tombstones are perhaps more eye-catching than the church in this photograph.

▼ **THURMASTON**
Newark Road c1965 T235015

A Roman milestone was excavated at Thurmaston, but the name is Anglo-Scandinavian. The village sits astride the Roman Fosse Way, but it is attractive no longer: for the last hundred years it has been in all but name a part of North Leicester. The relatively narrow main street carried heavy traffic to Nottingham, the north, and the east coast. By the late 1950s it had become overwhelmed, and Newark Road, known as the bypass, was constructed on the east side of the village. When this photograph was taken, the road had been open for two years, an arid, treeless swathe, but manna from heaven in an urgent world.

▶ **THURMASTON**
Melton Road c1965 T235008

The parish church of St Michael sits behind the buildings on the left of the now peaceful main street. Canal Street, Wharf Street, and Mill Lane on the right run back to the river. Left alone, the buildings in Melton Road could have reverted to a village atmosphere, but the Council in its usual insensitive manner authorised the demolition of the cottages on the left, and the erection of an amazingly ugly knitwear factory. As usual, the double-glazing salesmen have paid the street a visit!

◄ THURMASTON
The River Soar
c1965 T235002

The river weaves its way southwards from the pastures of Quorn and Cossington into the almost solidly developed northern edge of the city between Birstall to its west, and Thurmaston to its east. In 1965, there were just a few hopeful fishermen here, and some neglected boats, but now the area has been transformed into Watermead Country Park, with its marina, golf range, sports grounds and fishing.

MARKET HARBOROUGH AND THE SOUTH-EAST

BILLESDON
Front Street, now Church Street c1955 B593005

This tree-shrouded view shows the junction of Front Street with Back Street, now Brook Lane, curving left at the south end of the village. To the right, steps lead up to the 13th-century church of St John the Baptist. The tower and fine broach spire were accurately rebuilt by Kirk & Parry of Sleaford, Lincolnshire in 1861. The gable end of the single-storey Old School of 1650 (centre) is an important educational survival. Much vernacular architecture survives in the village, which will certainly reward the traveller with its variety of building materials and designs. North of the village is Billesdon Coplow, a prominent Leicestershire landmark, with close by, Botany Bay fox covert, dating from around 1788, the time of the infamous Australian Penal Colony.

KINGS NORTON, *The Church of St John the Baptist c1955* K129001

This superb Ketton stone-faced Gothic Revival church was built at the cost of just over £20,000 in just over one year, apart from the spire, for Squire William Fortrey by local architect John Wing (1728-94) of North Luffenham, Hallaton and finally Bedford. The spire was completed in 1775 but lost in a storm in 1850. From the south the full beauty of the church can be seen as it floats above the fields. The interior has hardly changed: the central three-decker pulpit, box pews and west gallery remain in situ in a wonderful airy space lit by clear windows. Outside at its east end is Wing's monument to William Fortrey, and close by is the 17th-century Fortrey manor house.

COUNTESTHORPE
The Square 1960
C471009

Countesthorpe, 'Cuntastorp' in 1242, has ballooned in recent decades to accommodate Leicester's commuters. Few early buildings remain in the village pre-dating the Enclosure Act of 1767, which destroyed the open field landscape so beloved by John Clare, the Northamptonshire poet. The black and white timbered house (right), on the corner of Green Lane and close to the parish church, is probably the earliest vernacular survival.

▼ **COUNTESTHORPE,** *Dale Acre c1965* C471016

Dale Acre opens directly into Central Street and Church Street, the village centre. The bungalows lack any architectural quality; it is the backdrop to the photograph which is of interest. Powered hosiery machines developed in the 1870s, and boiler-house chimneys such as those seen here attest to the village's industrial character. Of course, it paid the hosier to remove to Countesthorpe or Fleckney, where cheaper labour meant additional profit, and he is hardly going to worry that the village may become depressing and lacklustre.

▶ **COUNTESTHORPE**
St Andrew's Church
c1965 C471011

The church is at the original heart of this sprawling village. Its battlemented tower is the complete surviving remnant of the medieval church. The remainder of this oddly proportioned building was designed or altered by Henry Goddard (1793-1868), a prolific Leicester architect, in the early 1840s. His rather more talented son, Joseph (1840-1900), became his partner in 1862, and was responsible for the city's Clock Tower among other Leicester buildings.

◄**COSBY**
Main Street c1965
C433006

The camera looks towards The Nook, highlighting the frustration of what might have been. The arid area of grass, and the 1950s housing, could, with more lightness of touch, have provided a more welcoming entrance to the village from the north. Little has happened here since 1965, except that the spindly trees on the right have matured, and the Huntsman (previously the New Inn, centre left) has been rebuilt in a bland red brick. In 1615 the vicar complained that he could not support his family on a wage of under £5 a year; now, I feel that it is the very fabric of the village that seems to echo his sentiments.

► **COSBY**
St Michael's Church c1965 C433004

At the southern end of this expanded village, the church with its elegant spire dates for the greater part from the earlier 15th century. An oddity is the large external projection which houses the rood loft staircase; evidence suggests that the fabric of the chancel may predate the body of the church. How sad that God's breath will not be allowed to ripple the grassy sepulchral mounds of generations of villagers in this chaste churchyard.

▶ **BROUGHTON ASTLEY**
The Stream c1960
B517007

The village has been given a sweeping bypass, Broughton Way, on its north side, reducing the volume of traffic negotiating Main Street and the area around St Mary's Church and Old Mill Road. The photograph looks south-east along the culverted stream bordering Station Road, with housing of the 1920s and 30s on the extreme right. It is a great pity that a little more money could not have been found in the Council's coffers to provide a scheme of enhancement, rather than this concrete and iron piping solution.

◀ **BROUGHTON ASTLEY**
Ye Olde Bulls Head Inn c1960 B517005

The pub fronts Main Street, sitting prominently at the junction of Cosby Road and Station Road, and appears to be the bad conversion of a former row of cottages. The fake timber framing is ill considered and out of place, while the rear extension leaves much to be desired. The village along Main Street possesses no outstanding architecture. The Baptist chapel at nearby Sutton-in-Elms and an adjacent 17th-century farmhouse are, however, of some interest.

▲ **BROUGHTON ASTLEY,** *The War Memorial c1960* B517006

The archetypal memorial is sited at the junction of Frolesworth Road and Station Road, offering a permanent reminder of the inevitably sad consequences of war. The surroundings are fairly bleak, with two circular flowerbeds in close-cropped grass and two rather uncomfortable park bench seats.

◀ **BITTESWELL**
The Green c1960
B584006

The camera looks north towards the large green; on its right is the three-storey early 19th-century red brick Royal Oak pub. On the extreme right is St Mary's Church of 13th-century date with its stumpy recessed steeple. Several early 19th-century houses group around The Green, and in the mid l9th century the village was described as large.

▼ **BITTESWELL,** *The Old Smithy c1960* B584015

The advent of the internal combustion engine saw the demise of the village blacksmith, although the art is making something of a comeback with the demand for decorative railings and gates. It would be very difficult as a passer-by to identify this building as the former smithy. The conversion has obliterated any evidence of its former life, which has been replaced by a comparatively antiseptic look with shutters and flowerbeds.

► **BITTESWELL**
Russett Cottage c1960
B584020

This is an almost ideal two-storey chocolate box cottage, with its thatched roof and door hood, small pane timber casement windows, and a profusion of flowers and creepers adorning the boundary fence. The cottage was originally semi-detached, but the second entrance door has been blocked, and a window substituted. The 20th century has arrived at Russett Cottage with its telephone lines and unattractive television aerial.

◄ BITTESWELL
St Mary's Church
c1960 B584012

St Mary's with its late 13th-century tower dominates the east side of the village green. On the south side of the tower is a recess which may once have held a monument. The remainder of the church is dull, but the north transept was added in 1852 by William Parsons (1796-1857), an interesting local architect. In 1825 he designed Leicester Gaol, and the now-demolished Theatre Royal, Leicester, with Samuel Beazley in 1836. He also designed the Leicestershire and Rutland Lunatic Asylum (1837), now part of the Leicester University campus. Parsons was born at Scraptoft and educated at Billesdon School.

► SWINFORD
The Village c1965 S549007

Very close to Junction 19 on the M1 motorway, the village is unremarkable. The church is of the 13th century, but more interesting is the altar tomb to William Staresmore, its mid l8th-century vicar, who died falling into his pond; his will included 200 pickaxes, 240 razors, and 500 pairs of boots - eccentric or what? The photograph shows one of several good 18th-century brick houses to be found in the village. The 1930s saw the demolition of a number of picturesque cottages to make way for less attractive replacements, particularly in Fir Tree Lane, once called Dog Lane.

SWINFORD
All Saints' Church
c1965 S549006

In a picturesque setting of mature trees and a grassy churchyard, the building is in the main of the 14th century, apart from its two-bay 13th-century nave arcade. Even with its spikey pinnacles, the tower is unremarkable. The east end has been worked over more than once, firstly rebuilt in 1778, and then again in 1895.

SWINFORD, *Stanford Hall and the Lake c1965* S549004

We are in the extreme southern tip of the county: whilst Stanford Hall is in Leicestershire, the parish church and the village are in Northamptonshire. Pevsner rightly refers to the house (extreme left) as the finest of its date in the county, designed by William Smith of Warwick in 1697 for Sir Roger Cave. His brother, Francis Smith, designed the stable block (centre left) in 1737. Although they formed a prolific design partnership, William was trained as a bricklayer, and his brother as a stonemason. Among their other achievements were Cholmondeley Hall, Stoneleigh Abbey and Sutton Scarsdale.

SADDINGTON
Main Street c1955
S844005

This is a small hilltop village about a mile to the south east of expanding Fleckney. To its south is Saddington Reservoir, a picturesque stretch of water created in the 1790s to feed the Grand Union Canal. At about the same time, navvies were pushing through Saddington Tunnel on the canal. There are several nice late 18th- and early 19th-century houses in the village, such as the one facing the camera. The camera proves to be a magnet to two small boys (extreme right).

SADDINGTON, *St Helen's Church c1955* S844004

Situated on the south-west side of the village, the church was heavily restored by Frederick Peck of Maidstone in 1872. The building is of about 1300 with an unbuttressed west tower of 1707, when its spire was taken down. As a church architect, Peck was certainly indifferent, but his memorial is the former Royal Agricultural Hall, London Borough of Islington, which he built in 1861. It was converted in 1983, and is now the Business Design Centre.

FLECKNEY
High Street c1960
F134018

'The good, the bad and the ugly' is a phrase which springs to mind here. W G Hoskins refers to Fleckney as 'a large and dreary industrial village', but I would hesitate to agree entirely. A hosiery village it might have been, but the High Street retains much of the quiet charm shown in the photograph. Brookside (right) is abutted by a decent brick-fronted house with its later bungalow shop. It is here that the ugly appears, in the form of a hot red brick building (probably of the 1970s or 80s) in use as a Baptist church, totally obliterating the lane. Were no voices raised in protest when this building was submitted to the local Planning Committee?

► **FLECKNEY**
Saddington Road c1955
F134002

When factories arrived in the village in the 19th century, development along the Wistow, Saddington and Kilby Roads was inevitable. The red-brick solidity of the houses presents an almost urban face, apart from the small front gardens. Many houses have date plaques, and most fall into a range between 1890 and 1910. An off-licence offers Phipps ales and stout, and at the end of the row, as if anticipating further expansion, there is a small shop.

◄**FLECKNEY**
The Grand Union Canal c1965 F134022

The locks at Fleckney are a part of the descent of the canal from its high point at Foxton into the Soar Valley. The Union Canal Bill was approved by Parliament in 1793, and work began in 1794, reaching Fleckney in 1796. The canal bypasses Fleckney on its eastern side; the photograph looks north east across Second Lock, towards Kibworth bridge and Bridge House, as the waterway winds towards Newton Harcourt and South Wigston.

▲ **KILBY,** *Main Street c1965* K125003

Kilby is a Scandinavian form of the Old English 'cilda-tun'; the first part means 'child', or more probably 'young nobleman'. This small village is set in an enclosure landscape of straight hawthorn hedges, between Fleckney and Countesthorpe, to the south of the city. The unprepossessing church of St Mary Magdalen by Henry Goddard (1813-99 - see St Andrew's, Countesthorpe) sits on the south side of the main street. This view looks at what amounts to 19th-century small-scale development along the Fleckney Road; the whole adds up to a very cordial rural scene, common over southern Leicestershire.

◀ **KIBWORTH BEAUCHAMP**
The Square c1955 K119024

The parish of Kibworth originally bracketed together Kibworth Beauchamp, Kibworth Harcourt and Smeeton Westerby, sharing the mother church of St Wilfrid. The name Beauchamp derives from Walter de Beauchamp, lord of the manor in c1130. The square, originally Cross Bank, was bypassed in 1810 on its eastern side by the A6 Market Harborough to Leicester road. A red brick village, it has a number of good vernacular houses. Those in the photograph demonstrate the restrained quality of its late Georgian architecture.

KIBWORTH BEAUCHAMP
Fleckney Road c1955
K119004

The change in house types from the 19th century to the 1930s marks the expansion of the village along the road to Fleckney, itself an important hosiery and knitwear centre. The small, two-storey factory site on the left was, in all probability, bought cheaply by an enterprising Leicester businessman, and the fact that it was considerably extended points to his having some success. The two cars are superb examples of their period.

KIBWORTH BEAUCHAMP, *The Grammar School, School Road c1955* K119010

This was one of the finest grammar schools in Leicestershire. The photograph shows the rear of the red brick Master's House of c1725 (originally of two storeys, a third was added around 1835), backed by a neat garden and the tennis courts. In 1965 Anthony Crossland, Secretary of State for Education, made it his policy to destroy every grammar school in England, Wales and Northern Ireland. Leicester and Leicestershire were pleased to comply with such a destructive procedure. The Master's House is now a well-ordered private residence, and the gardens have suburban fencing divisions. The tennis courts are a car park!

KIBWORTH HARCOURT
Albert Street c1955 K171030

Harcourt is taken from Harcourt in Normandy, and from Roger de Harewecurt, who held the village in 1202. Until the A6 was pushed between the two villages, it made its way via their narrow rather tortuous streets. At the end of the 20th century, unfortunate changes were inflicted on this view. The houses on the left have been altered in a reasonably complimentary manner, but to the right the mature trees have gone, and the 18th-century garden wall has been mostly demolished to form a new entrance to the Old House. Beyond, an enclave of unspectacular houses has been built - not a happy transformation.

KIBWORTH HARCOURT, *The Old House, Main Street c1955* K171028

The Old House (left) dates from 1678, and it is a prominently sited example of English domestic architecture at its very best. It is a double-pile brick building with five bays of cross casement windows and stone dressings. The Parker coat of arms ornaments the broken scrolled pediment. Two oeil-de-boeuf windows and a later Tuscan-columned porch complete this quite picturesque ensemble.

KIBWORTH HARCOURT
Main Street c1960 K171046

This is red brick village Leicestershire at its best: nothing ostentatious in either the well-designed row of cottages (right) terminated by the Three Horseshoes pub, small and welcoming, or in the earlier farm group on the left. Although this must be part of a designated Conservation Area, it is so often fertile ground for the bonus-earning double glazing salesmen, who will assure the householder, without batting an eyelid, that he or she will 'never notice the difference' between the original timber sashes and casements and his plastic ones.

SMEETON WESTERBY, *Westerby Corner c1955* S742008

This attractive village retains its quiet rural atmosphere; it is ranged along its north-south street about a mile to the south of Kibworth Beauchamp. A semi-detached house of little architectural merit dominates the view here, but beyond is a glimpse of the Gumley Hills as the road swings right towards Saddington.

SMEETON WESTERBY
Christ Church c1955 S742007

The village lies some eight miles south of the city. The small church of 1849 was designed in a 14th-century manner by Henry Woodyer (1816-96), who worked briefly with William Butterfield. He was a Gothic Revival architect whose finest works included the House of Mercy, Windsor, and the Church of the Holy Innocents, Higham, Gloucestershire. How sad, then, that Christ Church, whilst pretty, cannot be said to be of great architectural moment. In fact, the west end (which we see here) gives the false impression that the grand nave arch has been blocked following the demolition of more substantial fabric.

FOXTON, *The Locks c1955* F159010

Foxton is a large village some 2½ miles north-west of Market Harborough, with the locks a further ½ mile to the west. There are few buildings of architectural merit, but the church of St Andrew, mainly of the later 13th century, is of interest: a priest was recorded here at Domesday, and a fragment of a Saxon cross shaft survives. The flight of locks was completed in 1812 descending 75 feet, comprising two staircases each of five narrow locks. The locks are out of shot, running up behind the lock-house to the right.

▶ **FOXTON**
*The Grand Union
Canal c1955* F159002

Silhouetted against the skyline, the south lock-house does not immediately appear to be a part of one of the county's major tourist attractions. A museum has opened on the site presenting a comprehensive history of the locks, and the Foxton Inclined Plane Trust hopes one day to reconstruct the lost building; but as in most similar projects, money might well prove to be the stumbling block.

◄ FOXTON
The Grand Union Canal c1960 F159104

The building to the right has been smartened up since 1955, and now advertises itself as Foxton Boat Services, providing boat trips and hire. Today it has doubled in size. Two heavily laden small craft are ready to set sail (centre). Supplying water to the locks was always difficult, and in 1910 an inclined plane designed by Gordon Cale Thomas was opened to ease the situation; however, it was expensive to operate, and was demolished in 1928.

▲ **GREAT EASTON**
The Village c1960 G198001

Great Easton lies in the south-east corner of the county, to the south of Eye Brook Reservoir, and to the north of industrial Corby, on the very edge of the Welland Valley. In an area of architectural gems (Rockingham Castle, Lyddington Bede House and Stoke Dry parish church), the village has a number of good ironstone houses of the 16th, 17th and 18th centuries arranged around two greens. The photograph, looking north towards Stockerston, focuses on the war memorial cross which is unhappily 'protected' by standard hairgrip railings.

▶ **DETAIL FROM** G198001

GREAT EASTON, *St Andrew's Church c1960* G198002

On the east side of the village, overlooking the Welland Valley, the church for the most part dates from the 13th and 14th centuries, including the tower and its broach spire. Ewan Christian, a rather dreary architect, rebuilt the spire in exact facsimile during his restoration work of 1864. A panelled Jacobean pulpit survives, and so does a somewhat eroded 14th-century monument.

THE COUNTY OF RUTLAND

CALDECOTT
High Street c1955 C468004

Apart from Rockingham, Caldecott is the only village on the north-south A6003 road between Uppingham and Corby. Prior to Dr Beeching's scything cuts, it had its own small railway station on the LM & SR Rugby and Peterborough line. The name translates literally as 'cold huts', or perhaps more probably to Cold Harbour, 'a place of shelter for wayfarers'. It is now a village of attractive 17th- and 18th-century houses, and the mason's imaginative use of stone is to be seen in the limestone-ironstone banding on some of the buildings.

CALDECOTT
High Street c1955 C468005

Roman remains are extant at Caldecott, but it is the later thatched and slated farmhouses, and rows of cottages (some with date panels) fronting onto the High Street which present a unified entity. The White Hart pub (centre right) sits at right angles to the street, but the inevitable 20th-century interloper of considerably lesser architectural merit can be seen in the distance. The base of a cross known as the Kingstone survived into the 20th century, but was removed and used as walling in Black Horse Lane. To the north of the village are earthworks, all that remains of the lost hamlet of Snelston.

CALDECOTT, *The Village c1955* C468008

The view is dominated by a fine 17th-century stone-faced house of two bays under a stone-slated roof, with substantial end stacks. The lower, later wing has been given a modern door. At a distance is the ironstone church of St John Evangelist with its Weldon stone steeple, rebuilt in 1797 after being struck by lightning. In the main, the building is of the 13th and 14th centuries, but it was very heavily restored in 1865, and in 1978 a rare 15th-century sanctus bellcote was removed after it was damaged.

SEATON
All Hallows' Church c1955 S547002

Seaton is situated on Rutland's south-eastern edge, about half a mile from its border with Northamptonshire, overlooking the Welland Valley. It is the 12th- and 13th-century work which raises All Hallows' above the ordinary, but the restoration of 1874 by the uninspired Cambridge architect W M Fawcett did little to enhance the interior. The east window of 1899 by Heaton, Butler & Bayne is worthy of note. They rank among the great stained glass makers and designers of the late 19th and early 20th centuries, including Kempe & Co, Morris & Co, and a particular favourite of mine, the Arts and Crafts designer Louis Davis. Externally, the 13th-century tower and broach spire are of extremely high quality.

SOUTH LUFFENHAM, *St Mary's Church c1955* S486003

This is a beautiful photograph of Rutland at its best. Pollarded willows line the stream, which appears to have trapped the wheels from a large cart. The curving footpath was probably on the original road line from Pilton to Barrowden. The setting of the 14th-century battlemented tower and its crocketed recessed steeple is ideal. Internally, the church has a good late 12th-century north arcade and a later south arcade. The great Gothic Revival architect George Edmund Street (1824-81) restored the building in 1852 and 1861.

SOUTH LUFFENHAM
The Village c1955 S486002

South Luffenham on the river Thater is a 7th-century Saxon settlement with North Luffenham, now adjacent to the A6121 Uppingham to Stamford road to the north, an attractive village of narrow streets and good limestone houses. St Mary's Church, with a very fine two-bay 12th-century north nave arcade, lies to the south-east, along with the rectory and the Hall. This later 17th-century house is unattributed, but it does have much in common with Lyndon Hall, designed by John Sturges in 1668. The photograph shows the entrance to the village across the stream, which is not improved by a pierced concrete Council parapet.

SOUTH LUFFENHAM, *The Boot and Shoe c1955* S486005

This is an almost idyllic scene, apart from the telegraph pole. The house, probably of the 18th century, with its mix of thatch and stone slates, fine gate piers, and a less substantial gate, masks the Boot and Shoe. The inn sign advertises Melbourns Fine Ales from a Stamford brewery no longer brewing, but retaining a number of tied houses supplied by Samuel Smith Old Brewery at Tadcaster, North Yorkshire.

EMPINGHAM
Crocket Lane c1960
E134009

The large very attractive Saxon village on the road from Oakham to Stamford now overlooks the modern dam on the north-east angle of Rutland Water formed in the valley of the River Gwash, landscaped by Dame Sylvia Crowe in the 1970s. Always of some local importance, the village had a weekly medieval market and three-day fair at the feast of St Botolph, granted in 1318. Although the photograph captures a cosy enclave of stone and thatched cottages, the village has expanded, and now contains a whole range of architectural styles.

▼ **EMPINGHAM,** *St Peter's Church c1960* E134014

This superb large church stands to the south of the village raised above the Stamford Road as it runs down to the later 17th-century Church Bridge over the River Gwash. It is said that a chapel of St Botolph once stood on the north side of the village, while on the north side of the parish was the now-deserted hamlet of Hardwick. Originally of the 12th century, the church was developed and altered each century up to the 15th. The remarkable 12th-century south doorway has carved jambs and a figure of Christ flanked by angels in the tympanum. What a pity that the nave is seriously marred by bad modern seating.

► **EMPINGHAM**
*Highfield
Close c1960*
E134005

A great field tree survives in this rather dreary comment on the quality of mid 20th-century domestic architecture. Concrete tiles, soldier arches and stretcher-bond brickwork combine in this aesthetic desert. There is nothing more to add.

◄ **COTTESMORE**
The Village c1955
C434007

The attractive stone built village stands on high undulating ground some four miles north-east of Oakham. Enclosed in 1800, the parish was in 1955 divided fairly evenly into arable and permanent grassland. Until 1928, when it was burnt down, the Hall stood at the east end of the village. The photograph selects a typical stone and thatch farmhouse group of the 17th and 18th centuries bounded by stone walls and picket fencing. A hospital of St Giles is mentioned here in 1266.

► **COTTESMORE**
The Village c1955 C434003

Here is a village at ease with itself, in the heart of stone country. On the extreme right is a single-decker bus which would now be an asset to any transport collection. The church of St Nicholas retains remnants of its Norman origins, but the fabric is mainly of a period around 1300, including the tower and tall broach spire. The great Victorian architect William Butterfield (1814-1900) rebuilt the south porch in 1851, and minor works were carried out here by the equally eminent John Loughborough Pearson (1817-97) in 1866.

► **LANGHAM**
*The School and School
Lane c1955* L337004

There are two prominent
buildings of quality in the
village, firstly the 13th-century
parish church of St Peter and
St Paul, and Langham Old Hall
with its date stone of 1665 built
into the south wall. The will of
Henry Forster dated 26 August
1692 directed that a school
master at £10 per year be
appointed at five Rutland
villages, including Langham, to
educate poor children free of
cost. By 1907 the building in the
photograph, which resembles a
country railway station, had on
average 108 pupils.

◄ COTTESMORE
The Sun Inn c1955
C434005

This wonderfully atmospheric pub, now an Everards house, is photographed before the universal advent of lager and 'Kids Welcome'. Its white-painted stone under a thatched roof is pierced by Norfolk sashed windows with extremely meagre-looking timber lintels. It is easy to imagine the Cottesmore hounds in front of the building. Established at Exton in 1732, the Cottesmore (one of England's premier hunts) moved to the village in 1740, having been bought by Sir William Lowther. Pressure groups may soon consign this country tradition to the history books.

▲ **LANGHAM,** *Cold Overton Road c1955* L337003

In the main, this is a large red-brick village, but a few thatched stone cottages remain, as in the photograph - note its superb hedges and simple topiary. Ranksborough, to the west of Langham, is the most famous of the Cottesmore hunt coverts, looking out over the choicest pastures and flying-fences. The area was brought vividly to life in 'Market Harborough', George Whyte Melville's sporting novel published in 1861. Prominent on the south side of the village in 1955, Ruddles Brewery, founded in 1858, was producing fine real ales, but in 1986 it was sold to Watneys, eventually to be absorbed into the Grand Metropolitan Group.

LOUGHBOROUGH AND THE NORTH-WEST

'This scene, how beauteous to a musing mind,

That now swift slides from my enchanted view;

The sun sweet setting yon far hills behind,

In other worlds his visits to renew.'

John Clare

'The Setting Sun' 1814

ANSTEY, *The Nook c1965* A312008

It is said that the first rumblings in Leicestershire of the Luddite Movement of c1815 were felt in Anstey with the breaking of the knitting machines. (Originating in Yorkshire, the movement is vividly painted in Charlotte Bronte's novel 'Shirley'.) Notwithstanding the Luddite threat, the village expanded rapidly to accommodate the influx of workers. The scene has changed little since 1965, apart from the demolition of the National Provincial Bank (right), to be replaced by an archetypal building of the late 1960s or early 1970s. It has to be said that The Nook is somewhat brighter than almost forty years ago.

ANSTEY
Bradgate Road c1965 A312011

The view shows the centre of Anstey, as the road drops down from the heights of Bradgate Park, enclosed out of Charnwood Forest c1200 as a hunting park. It was the birthplace of Lady Jane Grey, the ill-fated nine-days' queen, who was executed aged 17 in the Tower of London in 1554, the innocent victim of family ambitions. Much red brick building of the 19th century intruded into the village scene as industry spread from Leicester, including the impressive backdrop of factory buildings we see here. The village does retain some vestiges of its less recent past in a small collection of timber-framed houses.

ANSTEY, *The Pack-Horse Bridge c1960* A312004

On the south-east side of the village the five-arch stone bridge, perhaps of the 16th century, steps quietly across the very reedy Rotherby Brook. The view looks south-east towards the newly aligned A46 trunk road, with all its speed and noise. This was the original roadway into the village, now reduced in stature to a footpath, as the road now crosses the water to its north. This is a rather romantic monument to the past.

▼ **NEWTON LINFORD,** *The Village c1960* N96004

This photograph is dominated by a fine example of a stag-head oak, a normal condition, not a dying tree. The speed regulation signs do little to enhance an otherwise idyllic scene on the A50 Leicester-Coalville (Bradgate) Road, looking across to All Saints' Church, standing adjacent to the entrance to Bradgate Park. The church is comparatively plain apart from its large 15th-century traceried window on its south side. The Leicester architects Harry Roberts and John Woodhouse-Simpson added the north aisle and chancel in 1859.

▶ **SWITHLAND**
The Reservoir c1965
S550004

A mile or so south of Quorn, the camera looks north towards the weir, with Hawcliff Hill and Buddon Wood to the left. Behind the camera is the Leicester-Nottingham railway line, with Swithland village, better known for its slate quarries, sited at the south end of the water. The reservoir was created in 1896; it is one of four 19th-century artificial lakes in Charnwood Forest - the others are Thornton (1854), Cropston (1870) and Blackbrook (1906), all man-made but now an attractive, almost natural part of the country.

◀ ROTHLEY
Woodgate c1965
R259024

Rothley lies some five miles to the north of Leicester, and to the west of the busy A6. Although close to the River Soar, it was not until the arrival of the railway that it began to expand. The camera looks at the mundane, suburban face of the village as Woodgate drops down to Cross Green. The shop fronts in the left-hand row have retained much of their original quality, but Flair, the ladies' hairstylist (right), has made the alterations which were regrettably to become the hallmark of the decade. Even the car parking is beginning to lurch towards the need for yellow lines, and all that goes with them.

► ROTHLEY
Town Green c1965
R259019

We are south-west of the village centre, and the photograph exudes a strange feeling of well-cared-for neglect. The roadway, and the grass with its two forlorn seats and their single weakly tree, contrast with the well kept appearance of the surrounding houses. There are a number of timber-framed buildings in the immediate area; the box-framed 17th-century one (centre) is a good example.

► **ROTHLEY**
The Memorial
c1965 R259016

A sturdy compressed granite obelisk, prominently sited, every day forcibly relays its silent message to passers-by. Apart from the natural backdrop of trees, the setting is perhaps a little bleak.

◄ **ROTHLEY**
The Temple (the Rothley Court Hotel)
c1965 R259021

The Temple lies to the south-west of the village. Although land was granted to the Knights Templar around 1203, building did not start until 1231. The Templars were suppressed in 1312, and the Knights Hospitaller took over ownership. At the suppression in 1536, the Rothley estate moved into the hands of the Babingtons, whose relative, Anthony, hatched a subsequently failed Catholic plot to kill Queen Elizabeth I. The Temple as it stands is very much a multi-period house. The photograph shows the main front of c1600, and the Victorian additions of 1894 to the left. On the right is the original chapel of c1250, one of few survivals which include Temple Church, London, and Temple Balsall, Warwickshire.

▲ **ROTHLEY,** *The Temple, Rear Elevation c1955* R259004

The triple gables of the early 17th-century house form the centrepiece, with flanking wings. John Ely, a Manchester architect, added the Tudoresque bay window to the right in 1894. Thomas Babington Macaulay (1800-52), the historian and essayist, was born at the Temple on St Crispin's Day 1800, and it was his masterpiece 'The History of England', published between 1848 and 1862, for which he is most remembered.

◀ **ROTHLEY**
The Park c1955 R259009

A rough outfield, a pavilion with very few spectators in a tree-shrouded ground - this could be almost anywhere in England. Given a tough time by Edward III, but surprisingly not by James I and VI (1603-25) in his 'Book of Sports', cricket was in good health by 1700. Over-arm bowling arrived officially in 1864, and the first Test Match was played in Australia in 1877. It could be that the players in the photograph went on to bigger things, or maybe they played out the overs as solicitors or Council officials in the city.

▲ **DETAIL FROM** R259020

► **ROTHLEY**
The Church of
St Mary and St John
the Baptist c1965
R259020

This fine pink granite church, mainly of the 15th century, is well sited at the head of Church Street. Its solid clasping buttressed and battlemented tower rises in four stages. The building was restored in 1877 by the architect J Reynolds Rowe. It is rich in monuments, including one to Anne Babington (1648), attributed to Edward Marshall (1598-1675), whose monuments are of the first importance. He and his wife, Anne, had fourteen children, and his youngest, Joshua, carved a good monument to John Whatton in Leicester Cathedral. Outside the church are the remains of a 9th-century cross shaft, the largest in the county.

◄**WOODHOUSE EAVES**
Main Street c1955
W367049

The street rises away from the main village centre, past what is now the village hall (left). This attractive stone building is enhanced by its cast iron latticed windows and porch, both now gone. The character of the hall has been negated at a stroke, presumably because redecoration, both inside and out, required time-consuming but rewarding cleaning and repainting work, whereas the new windows require somewhat less effort.

◀ WOODHOUSE EAVES
Maplewell Road c1955
W367050

Local dry stone walling, brick and Swithland slate are all here in abundance, as the road drops down from Maplewell Hall to the village centre. Quarrymen and their families must have occupied a high proportion of the cottages, working to fulfil the 18th- and 19th-century demand for slate both as a roofing material, and for graveyard headstones, of which many are works of art. Ultimately the quarries were overwhelmed by the cheaper Welsh slate.

► **WOODHOUSE EAVES**
The View from the Rocks
c1960 W367075

This picturesque view across the village contrasts the rugged foreground with the domestic quality of the buildings, emphasising the fact that they sit on pre-Cambrian rocks, which are among the oldest in Britain. Since 1960 the view has lost some of its charm: the treed backdrop is now given over to a mass of small houses.

▼ **WOODHOUSE EAVES**
The View from the Memorial
c1955 W367039

The memorial stands against the sky looking out over Rushyfields to Woodhouse and Beaumanor Park. This pastoral scene suffers somewhat from the presence of a telegraph pole and its excessive number of wires.

► **WOODHOUSE EAVES**
Charnwood Forest, the Children's Convalescent Home
c1955 W367012

This large Edwardian house with its airy balcony and rows of timber sashed windows is on the south side of the village; it is just far enough from the city and high enough in the Forest to be beneficial. In 1955, when austerity was still a part of everyday life, this was as good as a holiday. To be ill as a child, a decade after the war, was considered worthwhile if it meant being allowed to recuperate at the Home. It was, however, just as good to return home again.

◄ **WOODHOUSE EAVES,** *St Paul's Church c1960* W367101

Seen here from the Swithland Road, the church, which is faced in slate from the local quarries, was designed in 1836 by William Railton (1801-77), a Gothic Revivalist and architect to the Ecclesiastical Commissioners. His finest work in Leicestershire was Beaumanor Park (1845), but his best known work is Nelson's Column. St Paul's was enlarged in 1870 and 1880, and the tower was rebuilt in 1904. In the foreground is the village's tribute to the fallen of two World Wars, admirably achieved with sensitivity and intimacy.

QUORN
Station Road c1965
Q11026

Here we see an attractive village centre group and a splendid single-decker bus. The battlemented tower of St Bartholomew's (left) just shows above the row of rather good brick and tile cottages, into which the post office has been thrust. Further along Station Road are a pretty thatched building, a good turn of the 19th century local granite house, and the 18th-century Dower House. It is interesting to contrast the fine street light on the left with the vision of things to come on the right. Behind it is an appalling flat-roofed modern intrusion.

► **QUORN**
Leicester Road
c1965 Q11015

Quorn ('Querendon' in 1209) means 'the hill from where millstones were obtained'. The village has acquired international fame as the home of the Quorn Hunt; its founder Hugo Meynell took residence in 1753 at Quorn Hall (now an educational centre). In this photograph the main road looks quiet, but traffic between Leicester and Loughborough would, in a few short years, build to a crescendo through the narrow streets. Now relief has come with the A6 bypassing the village. There have been losses, but the view remains recognisable.

◄ **QUORN**
The Bull's Head Hotel
c1960 Q11002

This is a mid 18th-century symmetrical brick building of quality, two and a half storeys high and five bays wide. A subsidiary wing has been added on the left, and further left are modern garages. The ground floor windows of the main block are later insertions, but the remainder appear to be original. Outside there is a fine array of contemporary cars, including a Morris Minor and a Ford Consul.

▲ **QUORN,** *St Bartholomew's Church c1960* Q11007

The church, mainly of the 14th century, stands within a grassy churchyard, close to the A6 Leicester-Loughborough Road. It is faced in hard, local Mountsorrel granite, with alterations and the addition of a north aisle by William Parsons in 1842 (see St Mary's, Bitteswell). The south aisle or Farnham Chapel contains monuments of interest, particularly one to John Farnham of Quorn Hall attributed to Epiphanius Evesham (1570-c1633), whose superb talent should have ensured his fame into the 21st century. Another example of his work is a monument to Lord Norris (1601) in Westminster Abbey and a lovely monument to Sir Thomas Hawkins in 1618 at Boughton-under-Blean, Kent.

◄ **KEGWORTH**
High Street c1960 K139005

The camera looks east down the High Street, which opens onto Church Gate and Derby Road. Kegworth's origins lay in its medieval weekly market and annual fair. The arrival of framework knitters heralded a dour expansion of red brick housing and hosiery factories, but some nice examples of vernacular architecture are to be found in the village. In the photograph, a butcher's shop front (left) with its rather flimsy canopy has been built into a rather good 17th-century cottage. Further on towards the parish church are a selection of early 19th-century houses, matched on the opposite side of the road by a later three-storey brick terrace.

▼ **KEGWORTH,** *Ashby Road c1965* K139016

Ashby Road becomes the High Street at the crossroads (centre); to the left is Packington Hill, and to the right Broadhill Road. Beyond the crossroads is the old village, with its three-storey, flat-fronted late 18th-century houses, while towards the camera the quality of the secondary layer of houses, including those of the 1930s on the right, deteriorates. A proliferation of television aerials never enhances the skyline.

▶ **KEGWORTH**

St Andrew's Church c1965
K139039

Dragwell, adjacent to A R Tarlton's chemist's shop (left), runs between Derby Road and Nottingham Road on the north side of the church, which stands prominently above the River Soar. It is said that the building, an almost perfect example of mid 14th-century work, was financed by Judge Sir Henry Greene, lord of the manor. The church is built of a grey sandstone; the scraping of the interior has left it somewhat dull, but relieved by the royal arms dated 1684 above the chancel arch. The church was restored in 1861 by Sheffield architect Joseph Mitchell.

◄**CASTLE DONINGTON**
Borough Street c1955 C430006

In the far north-west of the county, and almost in Derbyshire, this village must deserve small town status. The rare dedication of the parish church to St Edward King and Martyr gives a valuable clue to its pre-Conquest origins, referring as it does to the young King Edward who was murdered in 978 at the age of 16 by his brother Aethelred's supporters. The photographer stood with his back to the impressive medieval castle motte to look across The Hollow into Borough Street and the town, with its excellent array of mainly 18th-century and earlier buildings.

►**CASTLE DONINGTON**
High Street c1955 C430011

The leafy High Street rises away from the village to become the main road to Ashby-de-la-Zouch. In this peaceful scene, the fact that the village has a longstanding domestic industry tradition in framework knitting and basket making is not immediately apparent. In medieval times the town also supported the Hospital of St John the Evangelist, founded in 1189 for a chaplain and twelve poor people. To the right is the only visible building earlier than the 19th century, with its large timber-framed panels of the late 16th century. Further up the hill is Key House, a timber-framed building of some architectural merit, dated 1636.

97

▶ **CASTLE DONINGTON**
The Methodist Church c1955 C430013

Situated in Market Street and close to Apiary Gate, the church design echoes that of Non-conformist chapels up and down the country. It was designed in 1905 by Albert Edward Lambert in standard red brick Gothic style, as opposed to the Art Nouveau of his contemporary George Baines. A local architect, Lambert was quite versatile, designing the Albert Hall Methodist Mission in Nottingham (1909) in the form of a music hall, and Nottingham's Midland Station in a fashionable Edwardian manner.

▼ **MEASHAM**
The School c1965 M234008

In the mid to late 1950s, this pattern of school building was springing up everywhere. The standard plan puts the main entrance up two steps, with the assembly hall on the left under a low pitched roof, the boiler chimney in the middle, and classrooms to the right. Most of the building is under a flat roof, which doubtless very soon began to leak! Dustbins arranged along the front of the building might today be considered a health hazard. The Singer saloon and its counterpart, the Hillman Hunter, were two of the popular family saloons of the decade.

MEASHAM
Southern Counties Car Auctions
c1965 M234013

Basically a colliery village, Measham owes a small debt to businessman John Wilkes (1732-1805), who built warehouses by the canal as a distribution outlet and manufactured his own oversized bricks, known as 'Wilkes Gobs', in his local brickworks. His bricks were his reply to Government proposals to tax bricks after the costly War of American Independence in 1782. His warehouses survive, and so does part of his brickworks, and a single building from his cotton mill also survives in the car auction complex. Interestingly, the building was an outpost of cotton mills at Burton and Fazeley in Staffordshire, owned by the family of Prime Minister Sir Robert Peel. The car auctions were a magnet to young drivers from miles around looking for a good bargain.

MEASHAM, *Magna Motors of Measham Ltd c1965* M234014

This is not a beautiful scene, but some effort has been put into designing the brick boundary wall, flagpoles and railings. Behind is the car park for the cars to come under the hammer, and the fully mechanised tuning, repairing, and testing service of Magna Motors.

▼ IBSTOCK
The Crown Inn, Hinckley Road c1965 I48006

The road rises up from the south, past the parish church, to enter Ibstock, gateway to industrial north-west Leicestershire. The Crown Inn, a turn of the 20th century brick and tile pub, shows a friendly face to the traveller, offering Double Diamond; along with Watney's Red Barrel, it must be among the most over-advertised and over-rated beers ever.

► IBSTOCK
Station Road c1965
I48015

The back of the Crown Inn can just be seen in the centre, where Station Road becomes Hinckley Road, curving south past the parish church, and on to Nailstone and Market Bosworth. The original road to Market Bosworth bypassed Nailstone, following an ancient green lane to the west of Nailstone Gorse. The assemblage of 19th-century houses on the left is almost picturesque, looking out over open fields until the arrival of the houses on the right in the 1930s.

◀ IBSTOCK
High Street c1965
I48008

Some things never change: in a rather dull street of 19th- and early 20th-century buildings, on a Midland Red bus route, the Council is digging up the pavement! One oil lamp is their contribution to night time pedestrian safety. The village grew up in the Leicestershire coalfields, along with its neighbours Coalville, Ellistown and Bagworth. The discovery of a suitable brick-making clay in 1830 led to the opening of a second industry, which continues today.

▶ IBSTOCK
St Denys' Church c1965 I48004

The setting appears to be perfect: St Denys' is situated at the western end of a fine avenue of trees, close to its attractive 18th-century rectory. However, through the trees on the extreme left is the disruptive A447 Hinckley Road, with all its associated bustle and noise. The church is mainly of the 14th century, apart from the 15th-century clerestory and late 19th-century vestry. Extensive restoration works were carried out by Goddard and Paget (see St Andrews, Countesthorpe) between 1884 and 1900. Archbishop William Laud, Archbishop of Canterbury 1633-45, and supporter of King Charles I, was rector here for nine years.

HINCKLEY AND THE SOUTH-WEST

KIRBY MUXLOE
The Castle, Main Street c1965 K126008

In fact, the castle is a fortified manor house, carefully
set within a rectangular moat, and the beauty of the
remains resides not so much in the architecture as in
the glowing colour of the bricks, probably produced
close to the site under the supervision of John Eles.
Built by William Hastings, 1st Lord Hastings of Ashby-
de-la-Zouch around 1480, the castle matches in quality
the brickwork of the better-preserved Tattershall Castle,
Lincolnshire. While supporting Edward IV, Hastings
made enemies of the Woodvilles, and perhaps tried a
little too hard to push his personal ambitions. He was
executed on 13 June 1483.

▶ KIRBY MUXLOE

St Bartholomew's Church c1965
K126002

This is a pleasant enough small church, set as a church should be in grassy surroundings, well-populated by recumbent villagers. The body of the church is early 14th-century, but any patina of age was effectively neutralised by the restorations of 1849 and 1857. The added tower enhances the overall composition, but should the church be locked, do not embark on an extensive search for the key.

▼ GROBY

Leicester Road c1960 G220004

The A50 bypass now divides the village from its castle, of which only the motte survives; the remainder was demolished in the later 12th century. The local stone cottages in the lee of the tree-shrouded parish church (centre) rely on simple, but excellent, details for effect - no incongruous plastic windows and doors here. In front of the church is a three-storey tower which forms a part of the Old Hall. The modern expansion of Groby as a Leicester suburb can be seen on the left, as the road swings towards Coalville.

▼ **GROBY**
The Old Hall, Markfield Road c1960
G220002

The Greys of Bradgate fame and the Ferrars have lived at the Old Hall; Lady Elizabeth Ferrars married Sir Edward Grey, later Lord Ferrars. His son married Elizabeth Woodville, who went on to marry King Edward IV after she was widowed at the battle of St Albans in 1461. The photograph shows two parallel late 16th-century gabled blocks with large mullion and transom windows. Some fragments of the building may date to the ownership of the Greys.

GROBY
The Pool c1960 G220007

Before the birth of theme parks, a day out in the late 1950s (when comparatively few people owned a car) was by Midland Red bus to Groby Pool, Swithland Woods and Bradgate Park, with the statutory climb up to Old John. Once it was larger, but its 40 acres qualified the pool as the largest sheet of water in the county until the 19th century, hence the saying 'to thatch Groby Pool with pancakes' indicates any impossible undertaking. The photograph looks north, with Pool House glimpsed on the extreme right, while the granite quarries are beyond the trees.

▲ **TWYCROSS,** *The Village c1955*
T237001

The camera has been set up on a triangle of land at the junction of the A444 Burton Road with the road to Sheepy Magna, which drifts out of shot to the left. The houses of the late 18th and early 19th centuries are almost picturesque behind hedges and walls, with a restrained petrol sign being all that is needed to alert drivers to the garage's presence - petrol companies are now in the van of unbelievable garishness and visual offensiveness. Out of sight is the Curzon Arms Hotel.

► **DETAIL FROM** T237001

TWYCROSS
The Curzon Arms Hotel c1955
T237004

In 1955, the agitated ghost of Penn Assheton Curzon probably hovered over the site of Gopsal Park, the splendid house he inherited in 1773, unforgivably demolished in 1951. The architect was a local man, John Westley (1702-69), and the contract was completed by William and David Hiorns of Warwick. Almost opposite to the entrance to Gopsal Park stands the Curzon Arms, an altered late 18th-century brick and tile double-pile house. Atkinson of Aston, Birmingham, founded in 1855, did not emblazon the building with their logo. In 1959, the family sold out to Mitchells & Butler, a part of the giant Bass empire.

TWYCROSS, *The Village c1955* T237003

It is a quiet day in Twycross. The cafe is not overburdened with custom, and the road to the zoo, about two miles further on, awaits a surge of traffic, as does the Curzon Arms, at the road junction. The footpath between the low hedge and the rendered bungalow (right) offers a short meander to the gates of Gopsal Park and Little Twycross.

TWYCROSS *c1955*
T237007

The short battlemented tower adorns an attractive group of 18th- and 19th-century houses at the south-eastern end of the village. This is not a church to visit in search of an uplifting architectural experience, but the single east window is spectacular. Possibly given by William IV to the victor at the Glorious Fourth of June 1794, Earl Howe of Gopsal Hall, the medieval stained glass was assembled from various sources, including St Denis, the Sainte-Chapelle, and Le Mans Cathedral. Out of shot to the right is the former Old Hall, an excellent house of the early 18th century.

◄ **SAPCOTE**
The Post Office c1965
S485001

On the stony Stanton Road, Domesday Scepecote (meaning 'shelter for sheep') was home to the powerful Bassett family. A small medieval village with its almshouses of 1847 and school of 1819, it played an important part in the production of the original Red Leicester cheese. All this is now reduced to the anonymous, all-purpose architecture of the post office and similar expanding contemporary development, particularly on the north side of the village. The K6 telephone box (centre) is the design highlight.

◄ **BARWELL**
The Town Centre c1965 B525003

Industrialised Barwell is hardly a tourist Mecca, but the photograph clearly shows what a philistine Planning Committee can do to an essentially late 19th-century scene. Here is a roundabout with its carefully designed pinnacled central feature, and a number of two-storey domestic-scale buildings. Any collective visual quality that the earlier buildings may have had has been totally ruined by the overscaled, intrusive Co-operative House, with its so fashionable curtain walling of the late 1950s or early 60s. What do committees see when they look at proposal drawings?

◄ **SAPCOTE**
All Saints' Church and the Playing Field c1965
S485002

On the south side of the village, the playing fields lie to the north of Bassett Lane, running up to Hinckley Road. The church, originally 14th- and 15th-century, has been restored and restored again, especially in 1886 by W Bassett-Smith, who appears to have bad a series of minor commissions, which seem to have been executed with little success. Bassett Lane refers to Ralph Bassett, Lord Sapcote, supporter of Simon de Montfort (1208-65).

SAPCOTE
The Wesleyan Chapel c1965
S485006

On the east side of the village, this is an undernourished Non-conformist chapel, in a sense a poor relation of the Methodist church in Castle Donington. It is a turn of the 20th century brick Gothic building, erected to proclaim the teachings of John Wesley (1703-91), who founded Methodism, and his brother Samuel (1707-88), author of many fine hymns.

INDEX

Frith Book Co Titles

www.francisfrith.co.uk

The Frith Book Company publishes over 100 new titles each year. A selection of those currently available is listed below. For latest catalogue please contact Frith Book Co.
Town Books 96 pages, approximately 100 photos. **County and Themed Books** 128 pages, approximately 150 photos (unless specified). All titles hardback with laminated case and jacket, except those indicated pb (paperback)

Amersham, Chesham & Rickmansworth (pb)	1-85937-340-2	£9.99	Devon (pb)	1-85937-297-x	£9.99
Andover (pb)	1-85937-292-9	£9.99	Devon Churches (pb)	1-85937-250-3	£9.99
Aylesbury (pb)	1-85937-227-9	£9.99	Dorchester (pb)	1-85937-307-0	£9.99
Barnstaple (pb)	1-85937-300-3	£9.99	Dorset (pb)	1-85937-269-4	£9.99
Basildon Living Memories (pb)	1-85937-515-4	£9.99	Dorset Coast (pb)	1-85937-299-6	£9.99
Bath (pb)	1-85937-419-0	£9.99	Dorset Living Memories (pb)	1-85937-584-7	£9.99
Bedford (pb)	1-85937-205-8	£9.99	Down the Severn (pb)	1-85937-560-x	£9.99
Bedfordshire Living Memories	1-85937-513-8	£14.99	Down The Thames (pb)	1-85937-278-3	£9.99
Belfast (pb)	1-85937-303-8	£9.99	Down the Trent	1-85937-311-9	£14.99
Berkshire (pb)	1-85937-191-4	£9.99	East Anglia (pb)	1-85937-265-1	£9.99
Berkshire Churches	1-85937-170-1	£17.99	East Grinstead (pb)	1-85937-138-8	£9.99
Berkshire Living Memories	1-85937-332-1	£14.99	East London	1-85937-080-2	£14.99
Black Country	1-85937-497-2	£12.99	East Sussex (pb)	1-85937-606-1	£9.99
Blackpool (pb)	1-85937-393-3	£9.99	Eastbourne (pb)	1-85937-399-2	£9.99
Bognor Regis (pb)	1-85937-431-x	£9.99	Edinburgh (pb)	1-85937-193-0	£8.99
Bournemouth (pb)	1-85937-545-6	£9.99	England In The 1880s	1-85937-331-3	£17.99
Bradford (pb)	1-85937-204-x	£9.99	Essex - Second Selection	1-85937-456-5	£14.99
Bridgend (pb)	1-85937-386-0	£7.99	Essex (pb)	1-85937-270-8	£9.99
Bridgwater (pb)	1-85937-305-4	£9.99	Essex Coast	1-85937-342-9	£14.99
Bridport (pb)	1-85937-327-5	£9.99	Essex Living Memories	1-85937-490-5	£14.99
Brighton (pb)	1-85937-192-2	£8.99	Exeter	1-85937-539-1	£9.99
Bristol (pb)	1-85937-264-3	£9.99	Exmoor (pb)	1-85937-608-8	£9.99
British Life A Century Ago (pb)	1-85937-213-9	£9.99	Falmouth (pb)	1-85937-594-4	£9.99
Buckinghamshire (pb)	1-85937-200-7	£9.99	Folkestone (pb)	1-85937-124-8	£9.99
Camberley (pb)	1-85937-222-8	£9.99	Frome (pb)	1-85937-317-8	£9.99
Cambridge (pb)	1-85937-422-0	£9.99	Glamorgan	1-85937-488-3	£14.99
Cambridgeshire (pb)	1-85937-420-4	£9.99	Glasgow (pb)	1-85937-190-6	£9.99
Cambridgeshire Villages	1-85937-523-5	£14.99	Glastonbury (pb)	1-85937-338-0	£7.99
Canals And Waterways (pb)	1-85937-291-0	£9.99	Gloucester (pb)	1-85937-232-5	£9.99
Canterbury Cathedral (pb)	1-85937-179-5	£9.99	Gloucestershire (pb)	1-85937-561-8	£9.99
Cardiff (pb)	1-85937-093-4	£9.99	Great Yarmouth (pb)	1-85937-426-3	£9.99
Carmarthenshire (pb)	1-85937-604-5	£9.99	Greater Manchester (pb)	1-85937-266-x	£9.99
Chelmsford (pb)	1-85937-310-0	£9.99	Guildford (pb)	1-85937-410-7	£9.99
Cheltenham (pb)	1-85937-095-0	£9.99	Hampshire (pb)	1-85937-279-1	£9.99
Cheshire (pb)	1-85937-271-6	£9.99	Harrogate (pb)	1-85937-423-9	£9.99
Chester (pb)	1-85937-382 8	£9.99	Hastings and Bexhill (pb)	1-85937-131-0	£9.99
Chesterfield (pb)	1-85937-378-x	£9.99	Heart of Lancashire (pb)	1-85937-197-3	£9.99
Chichester (pb)	1-85937-228-7	£9.99	Helston (pb)	1-85937-214-7	£9.99
Churches of East Cornwall (pb)	1-85937-249-x	£9.99	Hereford (pb)	1-85937-175-2	£9.99
Churches of Hampshire (pb)	1-85937-207-4	£9.99	Herefordshire (pb)	1-85937-567-7	£9.99
Cinque Ports & Two Ancient Towns	1-85937-492-1	£14.99	Herefordshire Living Memories	1-85937-514-6	£14.99
Colchester (pb)	1-85937-188-4	£8.99	Hertfordshire (pb)	1-85937-247-3	£9.99
Cornwall (pb)	1-85937-229-5	£9.99	Horsham (pb)	1-85937-432-8	£9.99
Cornwall Living Memories	1-85937-248-1	£14.99	Humberside (pb)	1-85937-605-3	£9.99
Cotswolds (pb)	1-85937-230-9	£9.99	Hythe, Romney Marsh, Ashford (pb)	1-85937-256-2	£9.99
Cotswolds Living Memories	1-85937-255-4	£14.99	Ipswich (pb)	1-85937-424-7	£9.99
County Durham (pb)	1-85937-398-4	£9.99	Isle of Man (pb)	1-85937-268-6	£9.99
Croydon Living Memories (pb)	1-85937-162-0	£9.99	Isle of Wight (pb)	1-85937-429-8	£9.99
Cumbria (pb)	1-85937-621-5	£9.99	Isle of Wight Living Memories	1-85937-304-6	£14.99
Derby (pb)	1-85937-367-4	£9.99	Kent (pb)	1-85937-189-2	£9.99
Derbyshire (pb)	1-85937-196-5	£9.99	Kent Living Memories(pb)	1-85937-401-8	£9.99
Derbyshire Living Memories	1-85937-330-5	£14.99	Kings Lynn (pb)	1-85937-334-8	£9.99

Available from your local bookshop or from the publisher

Frith Book Co Titles (continued)

Title	ISBN	Price	Title	ISBN	Price
Lake District (pb)	1-85937-275-9	£9.99	Sherborne (pb)	1-85937-301-1	£9.99
Lancashire Living Memories	1-85937-335-6	£14.99	Shrewsbury (pb)	1-85937-325-9	£9.99
Lancaster, Morecambe, Heysham (pb)	1-85937-233-3	£9.99	Shropshire (pb)	1-85937-326-7	£9.99
Leeds (pb)	1-85937-202-3	£9.99	Shropshire Living Memories	1-85937-643-6	£14.99
Leicester (pb)	1-85937-381-x	£9.99	Somerset	1-85937-153-1	£14.99
Leicestershire & Rutland Living Memories	1-85937-500-6	£12.99	South Devon Coast	1-85937-107-8	£14.99
Leicestershire (pb)	1-85937-185-x	£9.99	South Devon Living Memories (pb)	1-85937-609-6	£9.99
Lighthouses	1-85937-257-0	£9.99	South East London (pb)	1-85937-263-5	£9.99
Lincoln (pb)	1-85937-380-1	£9.99	South Somerset	1-85937-318-6	£14.99
Lincolnshire (pb)	1-85937-433-6	£9.99	South Wales	1-85937-519-7	£14.99
Liverpool and Merseyside (pb)	1-85937-234-1	£9.99	Southampton (pb)	1-85937-427-1	£9.99
London (pb)	1-85937-183-3	£9.99	Southend (pb)	1-85937-313-5	£9.99
London Living Memories	1-85937-454-9	£14.99	Southport (pb)	1-85937-425-5	£9.99
Ludlow (pb)	1-85937-176-0	£9.99	St Albans (pb)	1-85937-341-0	£9.99
Luton (pb)	1-85937-235-x	£9.99	St Ives (pb)	1-85937-415-8	£9.99
Maidenhead (pb)	1-85937-339-9	£9.99	Stafford Living Memories (pb)	1-85937-503-0	£9.99
Maidstone (pb)	1-85937-391-7	£9.99	Staffordshire (pb)	1-85937-308-9	£9.99
Manchester (pb)	1-85937-198-1	£9.99	Stourbridge (pb)	1-85937-530-8	£9.99
Marlborough (pb)	1-85937-336-4	£9.99	Stratford upon Avon (pb)	1-85937-388-7	£9.99
Middlesex	1-85937-158-2	£14.99	Suffolk (pb)	1-85937-221-x	£9.99
Monmouthshire	1-85937-532-4	£14.99	Suffolk Coast (pb)	1-85937-610-x	£9.99
New Forest (pb)	1-85937-390-9	£9.99	Surrey (pb)	1-85937-240-6	£9.99
Newark (pb)	1-85937-366-6	£9.99	Surrey Living Memories	1-85937-328-3	£14.99
Newport, Wales (pb)	1-85937-258-9	£9.99	Sussex (pb)	1-85937-184-1	£9.99
Newquay (pb)	1-85937-421-2	£9.99	Sutton (pb)	1-85937-337-2	£9.99
Norfolk (pb)	1-85937-195-7	£9.99	Swansea (pb)	1-85937-167-1	£9.99
Norfolk Broads	1-85937-486-7	£14.99	Taunton (pb)	1-85937-314-3	£9.99
Norfolk Living Memories (pb)	1-85937-402-6	£9.99	Tees Valley & Cleveland (pb)	1-85937-623-1	£9.99
North Buckinghamshire	1-85937-626-6	£14.99	Teignmouth (pb)	1-85937-370-4	£7.99
North Devon Living Memories	1-85937-261-9	£14.99	Thanet (pb)	1-85937-116-7	£9.99
North Hertfordshire	1-85937-547-2	£14.99	Tiverton (pb)	1-85937-178-7	£9.99
North London (pb)	1-85937-403-4	£9.99	Torbay (pb)	1-85937-597-9	£9.99
North Somerset	1-85937-302-x	£14.99	Truro (pb)	1-85937-598-7	£9.99
North Wales (pb)	1-85937-298-8	£9.99	Victorian & Edwardian Dorset	1-85937-254-6	£14.99
North Yorkshire (pb)	1-85937-236-8	£9.99	Victorian & Edwardian Kent (pb)	1-85937-624-X	£9.99
Northamptonshire Living Memories	1-85937-529-4	£14.99	Victorian & Edwardian Maritime Album (pb)	1-85937-622-3	£9.99
Northamptonshire	1-85937-150-7	£14.99	Victorian and Edwardian Sussex (pb)	1-85937-625-8	£9.99
Northumberland Tyne & Wear (pb)	1-85937-281-3	£9.99	Villages of Devon (pb)	1-85937-293-7	£9.99
Northumberland	1-85937-522-7	£14.99	Villages of Kent (pb)	1-85937-294-5	£9.99
Norwich (pb)	1-85937-194-9	£8.99	Villages of Sussex (pb)	1-85937-295-3	£9.99
Nottingham (pb)	1-85937-324-0	£9.99	Warrington (pb)	1-85937-507-3	£9.99
Nottinghamshire (pb)	1-85937-187-6	£9.99	Warwick (pb)	1-85937-518-9	£9.99
Oxford (pb)	1-85937-411-5	£9.99	Warwickshire (pb)	1-85937-203-1	£9.99
Oxfordshire (pb)	1-85937-430-1	£9.99	Welsh Castles (pb)	1-85937-322-4	£9.99
Oxfordshire Living Memories	1-85937-525-1	£14.99	West Midlands (pb)	1-85937-289-9	£9.99
Paignton (pb)	1-85937-374-7	£7.99	West Sussex (pb)	1-85937-607-x	£9.99
Peak District (pb)	1-85937-280-5	£9.99	West Yorkshire (pb)	1-85937-201-5	£9.99
Pembrokeshire	1-85937-262-7	£14.99	Weston Super Mare (pb)	1-85937-306-2	£9.99
Penzance (pb)	1-85937-595-2	£9.99	Weymouth (pb)	1-85937-209-0	£9.99
Peterborough (pb)	1-85937-219-8	£9.99	Wiltshire (pb)	1-85937-277-5	£9.99
Picturesque Harbours	1-85937-208-2	£14.99	Wiltshire Churches (pb)	1-85937-171-x	£9.99
Piers	1-85937-237-6	£17.99	Wiltshire Living Memories (pb)	1-85937-396-8	£9.99
Plymouth (pb)	1-85937-389-5	£9.99	Winchester (pb)	1-85937-428-x	£9.99
Poole & Sandbanks (pb)	1-85937-251-1	£9.99	Windsor (pb)	1-85937-333-x	£9.99
Preston (pb)	1-85937-212-0	£9.99	Wokingham & Bracknell (pb)	1-85937-329-1	£9.99
Reading (pb)	1-85937-238-4	£9.99	Woodbridge (pb)	1-85937-498-0	£9.99
Redhill to Reigate (pb)	1-85937-596-0	£9.99	Worcester (pb)	1-85937-165-5	£9.99
Ringwood (pb)	1-85937-384-4	£7.99	Worcestershire Living Memories	1-85937-489-1	£14.99
Romford (pb)	1-85937-319-4	£9.99	Worcestershire	1-85937-152-3	£14.99
Royal Tunbridge Wells (pb)	1-85937-504-9	£9.99	York (pb)	1-85937-199-x	£9.99
Salisbury (pb)	1-85937-239-2	£9.99	Yorkshire (pb)	1-85937-186-8	£9.99
Scarborough (pb)	1-85937-379-8	£9.99	Yorkshire Coastal Memories	1-85937-506-5	£14.99
Sevenoaks and Tonbridge (pb)	1-85937-392-5	£9.99	Yorkshire Dales	1-85937-502-2	£14.99
Sheffield & South Yorks (pb)	1-85937-267-8	£9.99	Yorkshire Living Memories (pb)	1-85937-397-6	£9.99

See Frith books on the internet at www.francisfrith.co.uk

FRITH PRODUCTS & SERVICES

Francis Frith would doubtless be pleased to know that the pioneering publishing venture he started in 1860 still continues today. Over a hundred and forty years later, The Francis Frith Collection continues in the same innovative tradition and is now one of the foremost publishers of vintage photographs in the world. Some of the current activities include:

Interior Decoration

Today Frith's photographs can be seen framed and as giant wall murals in thousands of pubs, restaurants, hotels, banks, retail stores and other public buildings throughout the country. In every case they enhance the unique local atmosphere of the places they depict and provide reminders of gentler days in an increasingly busy and frenetic world.

Product Promotions

Frith products are used by many major companies to promote the sales of their own products or to reinforce their own history and heritage. Frith promotions have been used by Hovis bread, Courage beers, Scots Porage Oats, Colman's mustard, Cadbury's foods, Mellow Birds coffee, Dunhill pipe tobacco, Guinness, and Bulmer's Cider.

Genealogy and Family History

As the interest in family history and roots grows world-wide, more and more people are turning to Frith's photographs of Great Britain for images of the towns, villages and streets where their ancestors lived; and, of course, photographs of the churches and chapels where their ancestors were christened, married and buried are an essential part of every genealogy tree and family album.

Frith Products

All Frith photographs are available Framed or just as Mounted Prints and Posters (size 23 x 16 inches). These may be ordered from the address below. From time to time other products - Address Books, Calendars, Table Mats, etc - are available.

The Internet

Already fifty thousand Frith photographs can be viewed and purchased on the internet through the Frith websites and a myriad of partner sites.

For more detailed information on Frith companies and products, look at these sites:

www.francisfrith.co.uk
www.francisfrith.com
(for North American visitors)

See the complete list of Frith Books at:

www.francisfrith.co.uk

This web site is regularly updated with the latest list of publications from the Frith Book Company. If you wish to buy books relating to another part of the country that your local bookshop does not stock, you may purchase on-line.

For further information, trade, or author enquiries please contact us at the address below:
The Francis Frith Collection, Frith's Barn, Teffont, Salisbury, Wiltshire, England SP3 5QP.
Tel: +44 (0)1722 716 376 Fax: +44 (0)1722 716 881 Email: sales@francisfrith.co.uk

See Frith books on the internet at www.francisfrith.co.uk

FREE PRINT OF YOUR CHOICE

Mounted Print
Overall size 14 x 11 inches (355 x 280mm)

Choose any Frith photograph in this book.
Simply complete the Voucher opposite and
return it with your remittance for £2.25 (to cover
postage and handling) and we will print the
photograph of your choice in SEPIA (size 11 x 8
inches) and supply it in a cream mount with a
burgundy rule line (overall size 14 x 11 inches).
**Please note: photographs with a reference
number starting with a "Z" are not Frith
photographs and cannot be supplied under
this offer.**
Offer valid for delivery to UK addresses only.

PLUS: **Order additional Mounted Prints
at HALF PRICE - £7.49 each** (normally £14.99)
If you would like to order more Frith prints from
this book, possibly as gifts for friends and family,
you can buy them at half price (with no
additional postage and handling costs).

PLUS: **Have your Mounted Prints framed**
For an extra £14.95 per print you can have your
mounted print(s) framed in an elegant polished
wood and gilt moulding, overall size 16 x
13 inches (no additional postage and handling
required).

IMPORTANT!

**These special prices are only available if you use
this form to order . You must use the ORIGINAL
VOUCHER on this page (no copies permitted). We
can only despatch to one address. This offer
cannot be combined with any other offer.**

Send completed Voucher form to:
**The Francis Frith Collection, Frith's Barn,
Teffont, Salisbury, Wiltshire SP3 5QP**